Praise for Dr. Dee Carroll and
Emotional Emancipation

"For those struggling through adversity—self imposed or life imposed—*Emotional Emancipation* provides a clear-eyed roadmap back to freedom! If you need a kick in the pants to get up and get going again, this book can be a lifesaver! Dr. Dee nails it!"

—*Joe Coughlin, Owner, Coconut Joe's Restaurant and Catering*

"Dee's book clearly shows us how everything that happens is a gift, how adversity can make us magnificent creatures if we let it, and how embracing it can bring about an amazing journey of emotional healing and overall heath. I love this book."

—*Homayoun Sadeghi, MD*

Emotional Emancipation

Emotional Emancipation

Step Into Your Freedom, Reinvent Your Challenges, and Move Beyond

Dr. Dee Carroll

AlCinde Publishing

Editorial work and production management by Eschler Editing.
Cover design by Kimberly Kay Durtschi.
Interior print design and layout by Kimberly Kay Durtschi.
eBook design and layout by Marny Parkin.

Published by AlCinde Publishing

First Edition: July 2018
Printed in the United States of America

10 9 8 7 6 5 4 3 2

ISBN 978-1-7325159-0-1

Gratitude

To my dear and loving mother, "Cindy," who transitioned from this life into the next just a few months before this book was published. You were and still are my rock, foundation, and encouragement.

To my dad, Albert—your training and discipline kept me on the straight and narrow.

To my sister Veni—thank you for being there for me without hesitation.

To my siblings Al, Ree Ree, Alma, and William; godparents Pat and Daz; and other family, friends, and associates—I greatly appreciate your support throughout my journey.

To my aunts and uncles who helped shape my life: Essie, Reather, Rosa, Ernestine, Rebecca, Clara, Willie Mae, Mamie, James, and Moses—you blessed my life.

To my godbrother Rev. Gregory James who moved beyond life's adversities after facing devastating and overwhelming odds—you are an inspiration.

To my dear friend Rev. Dr. Leonard N. Smith and members of the clergy who have positively impacted my life.

Contents

Foreword

Twenty-eight years of my life, Dee Carroll thought with despair. *And it's all gone.* As her new reality sunk in—another failed marriage, the sale of her dream home, and the loss of her multimillion-dollar consulting business—Dee began to ask herself how she could possibly move forward.

She had no retirement savings left. Her investments were gone, too. She was depleted both financially and mentally. She was overwhelmed. And devastated.

When I first met Dee, she had come to me for help "reinventing" herself. She wanted to learn what she could from her recent experiences, but also leave them behind for good—emancipating herself from the agony and pain and heartbreak she had experienced. As we began to talk, I realized that she had already made a tremendous start—creating in the process a uniquely powerful formula that anyone could use to liberate themselves from their past, release the debilitating emotions, and recover their sense of purpose and self-worth. I was immediately taken with the idea that some could easily free themselves from the baggage that we so often carry forward into our future lives.

Emotional Emancipation is the playbook for reinventing yourself.

Moving you from agony to achievement, it details Dee's prescription to attain F.R.E.E.D.O.M.—breaking free from your past to restore your equilibrium and create the new life you want. With this book, you'll discover how to never again accept failure as a "normal" part of life.

Dee is a gifted speaker, a powerful coach, and a thoughtful and engaging seminar host.

Join me in learning to become emotionally emancipated and free to live a fuller life. Dee will position you to stay in the game and never accept quitting as an option.

—Jack Canfield

Introduction

Another book on adversity?

Hold on. First of all, this isn't a book on *adversity*. It's a book on how to bounce back from adversity. On how to use what you learn from adversity to make you stronger. To help you discover unique tools to liberate, release, recover, restore, and reinvent your life.

Because you need to know that. Each of us does. Because each of us will, at one time or another, stare adversity in the face.

And here's something you need to know before you read another word: I am *exactly* the right person to tell you all about how to rebound from adversity. Because I have stared adversity in the face. At one point I thought it had me—thought I'd never come out on the other side. But I asked God for grace, found the inner strength, grabbed adversity by the horns, and fought back.

What I learned in the process was priceless. And I want to share it with you.

Let me tell you what happened to me. It may not differ that dramatically from what has happened to you—not in the details, of course, but in the impact on your heart and soul.

Awhile back—before adversity reared its ugly head—I thought my life was just about as sweet as it was ever going to get. I owned a multimillion-dollar human resources and management consulting firm. After twenty-plus years of investing my all in its success, it was doing very well financially. So was I. My mom had moved in with me after the death of my father, and I was delighting in the opportunity to care for her. I was blessing others who were also part of my life. I lived in my dream home, and I was married to a man I adored.

I was on top of the world.

On top of the world, that was, except for a nagging feeling that something just wasn't right.

Day after day, week after week, I did battle with a gnawing feeling in the pit of my stomach that *something was wrong*. I couldn't put my finger on it. I couldn't put *anything* on it, for that matter. I simply couldn't grasp what might be giving me the feeling of dread that far too frequently snaked up my spine and made me so uneasy.

On the outside, everything seemed perfect. On the inside, my mind and spirit were waiting for the other shoe to fall.

I eventually figured out that it had to be financial. My inner spirit confirmed that suspicion and prompted me to check my books. To look at my numbers. To go over my dollars. So I did.

Afterward, I was more confused than ever. Everything looked fine—just as it should. But I couldn't shake the sick feeling that everything *wasn't* fine. I suddenly realized I hadn't seen a borrowing base certificate—what we used to draw down on the line of credit—for several weeks. In fact, it had been *more* than several weeks. That was unusual, and I called my CFO to ask about it.

He was calm, cool, and collected—and he had a ready explanation. "We are self-financing," he said.

The nagging feeling I'd had, the inner warning that something was wrong, lit up the night sky. Now I *knew* something was wrong. The timing didn't support the notion of "self-financing." We were embarking on the final quarter of the fiscal year, and I knew our clients wouldn't be paying that quickly right then. I knew we'd be relying on a line of credit to keep things going.

My next call was to my representative at the bank. I told him what the CFO had said. He didn't skip a beat before telling me that every two weeks, my company was presenting a borrowing base certificate and drawing down money.

I was dumbfounded. "On whose authority?" I stammered.

"Your CFO is processing and approving the documents," my bank rep told me.

How could that be? I had not given him approval to do any such thing.

Fast forward. One meeting followed another, and before long the CFO resigned. I prayed fervently that God would reveal the discrepancies before this man left the company. I needed to know exactly where we stood and what had happened.

When the CFO left that final meeting to write his statement of resignation, the controller handed me the latest financial reports. Remember, I had reviewed the numbers with a fine-tooth comb, as it were, and hadn't been able to identify the problem. This time, God answered my prayer. There, right before my eyes, was the obvious answer. More than $400,000 was unaccounted for. Divine assistance helped me see what I hadn't been able to before.

To the CFO's credit, he admitted his wrongdoing. He'd been keeping two sets of books. He hadn't updated the main system. He had misappropriated the money without me knowing and without anyone in the accounting department knowing.

I was shocked. This was a man I had trusted with my corporation's finances—with the very health and well-being of my company. His behavior impacted me, everyone who worked for me, and all the clients who trusted us.

When I asked the obvious—*How could you?*—he asked to speak with me in private. Walking to the window, he turned to face me. A tear slid down his cheek. "Dr. Carroll, I'm sorry. I'm so sorry. If there is anything I can do to help, I will."

A series of events was set in motion beyond all our ability to "help." The bank ordered a quarterly field audit, something that hadn't been done in more than a year. Following that, an outside CPA firm did a thorough review. To my horror, they discovered additional missing money, including almost a quarter of a million dollars in duplicate invoices.

Honor bound, I immediately paid those duplicate invoices back to the clients.

Ultimately, the bank called in my line of credit. Next, it refused to cover my payroll of $300,000. I filed Chapter-11 bankruptcy, structuring a repayment plan I hoped and prayed would end the nightmare once and for all. That's when I found out what a nightmare really was: the bank, my largest creditor, would not accept the plan. The Chapter-11 bankruptcy was dismissed. All the while, I bounced in and out of the emergency room, eventually undergoing major surgery, my flagging health no doubt compromised by the unrelenting stress.

My sweet life was unraveling at an astonishing speed, and I was rapidly running out of options.

Just before the Chapter-11 bankruptcy was dismissed, my law firm advised me to file a Chapter-7 bankruptcy. It would allow me to "start over." It was, they claimed, my only alternative.

I refused.

I felt a real obligation to my clients and employees. Filing a Chapter 7 would leave them all holding the bag, something I didn't feel good about. I convinced myself that as catastrophic as the situation was, I could pull it out if I just worked hard enough.

I had decided on an action plan but never got an opportunity to implement it when the bank—not only my largest but clearly most ferocious creditor—filed suit against me. When all was said and done, the bank was granted a judgment against me both professionally and personally. The result? My personal and business accounts were frozen. My hands were completely tied. I was, in effect, penniless.

There was no longer any question. No grasping at straws in a desperate attempt to make it work. I was *completely* out of options.

I dissolved my company—the one I had poured my whole soul into for twenty-eight years. I filed a Chapter-7 bankruptcy that covered me personally as well as professionally. By the time the dust settled, I'd lost my business, my savings, an investment apartment building, my marriage, and ultimately decided to walk away from my dream home.

I had lost it all. Everything. Or so I thought.

I spent many nights in bed, flat on my back, staring at the ceiling and crying until I was exhausted and no more tears would come. I felt during those moments that I had nothing to live for. Though my love and respect for God would never allow me to do such a thing, I finally understood why people are driven to suicide. My despair was dark—and while I *wanted* to climb out of the abyss, I didn't know how to take the first step.

It was then that a simple, seemingly insignificant conversation not only gave me the courage to take that first step but to set my life in a new and meaningful direction.

I had temporarily moved in with my sister. While I was grateful for her generosity, living together was a challenge. (You've heard the old adage that adults should have their own places? Boy, can I testify to that!) While I love my sister and will be forever grateful for her support and kindness, we were both desperate for a break. I pulled together the money to take a short cruise.

I signed up for several acupuncture treatments on the ship and confided some of my problems to the acupuncturist. During my last session, the acupuncturist asked, "What are you going to do with your life now?" When I told him I wasn't sure, he said, "Why not take a job on the ship? You could manage any of several departments. You're brilliant, and you obviously have what it takes to not only *get* a job but to excel at it."

Suddenly, a light bulb went off in my head.

That was me! I might have lost everything I had, but *I was still me*! I was still driven. I was still a rainmaker. I still had what it took to be whatever I chose!

I hadn't lost everything, after all. *I still had my mojo.*

Spoiler alert: I didn't take a job on the ship.

But I *did* reinvent myself.

The worst of the storm is behind me now, and I am excited about my future. And here's the best part about that: I can help *you* reinvent yourself. I can help you get excited about *your* future.

What my CFO did was criminally irresponsible. It could have ruined my life. It almost did. It was terrifying to walk away from what I believed were my best days. It was downright menacing to leave behind everything I knew. It was one of the most daunting things I have ever faced.

Maybe you have felt that way. Maybe you feel that way right now.

If so, here's what I want to share with you: Walking away from everything you know is *not* the end of your life. Everything that happens to you is a gift. Everything you go through can lead you to a new lease on life. And everything you face will prepare you in sublime ways for the amazing things to come.

Don't believe me? Maybe you can't believe that right now. But it's true. I know it's true because it happened to me. And if it happened to me, it can happen to you.

There is no doubt in my mind of that truth.

And because I have walked every step of that journey, I want to show you how to unlock that promise in your own life.

I know you can do it. Please allow me to walk it with you.

Chapter One

Emotional Emancipation: Free Yourself

*Lock up your libraries if you like; but there is no gate,
no lock, no bolt that you can set upon the freedom of
my mind.*

—Virginia Woolf

There are many ways to define freedom, but one of
my favorites—and one of the most compelling—was
offered by American historian Daniel J. Boorstin: "Freedom
means the opportunity to be what we never thought we would be."

I want to start the journey of reinventing adversity with what I
consider the foundation of that endeavor: the quest for emotional
emancipation, which results in a staggering sense of freedom that
liberates you to be what you never thought you would be. Because
when you discover what you can really be, there is a world of limit-
less possibility ahead of you—a world that far surpasses any adversity
you may be facing right now.

What does it mean to be free? It doesn't necessarily mean doing
whatever you want to do, but it *does* mean you know what to do

and what not to do. Being free means you are not controlled by society's labels of right or wrong but that you have the right to decide what is right or wrong for you. It means you are free to make your own decisions and that you can decide what makes you happy. It means you are free to control your destiny and free to commit to the processes and goals that will get you there. It means, really, that you are free to be *free*.

I call this kind of freedom *emotional emancipation* for an important reason. Throughout history, the word *emancipation* has been used to define the freeing of someone from slavery; in the United States, the document that officially ended the institution of slavery was called "The Emancipation Proclamation." But I'd like to suggest that there is a very different kind of "slavery" in which we can become confined, and that is the process of being bound by what others think we can be, do, or achieve. Sometimes it is being bound by the limits we ourselves impose. The ability to emancipate ourselves from that type of domination is every bit as critical—and every bit as much of a struggle—as the fight to free human beings from the ritual of slavery. As Albert Einstein said, "Everything that is really great and inspiring is created by the individual who can labor in freedom."

What, then, is *freedom*? I am not talking here about the political environment of a nation. I am talking about the status of an individual—the power or right to act, speak, or think as one wants without hindrance or restraint. U.S. president Herbert Hoover said, "Freedom is the open window through which pours the sunlight of the human spirit and human dignity." And Ralph Waldo Emerson pointed to its importance when he wrote, "For what avail the plough or sail, or land or life, if freedom fail?"

When I speak of freedom, I am also talking about the freedom to fail. There's a tendency to regard failure as the end of the world—a mistake from which we can never bounce back. In a state of emotional emancipation, there's a definite place for failure (something I'll talk about more in chapter 3). In so many ways, failure can actually propel you to success. As Mahatma Gandhi so wisely stated, "Freedom is not worth having if it does not include the freedom to make mistakes."

But what I'd like to emphasize most right now, especially as it pertains to the process of reinventing adversity, is the fact that true freedom is the power to change—to change your circumstances, your perceptions, your limitations, your potential. When you are truly emotionally emancipated, you will be empowered to change, and nothing will ever be the same again.

You will gain, for perhaps the first time in your life, the courage to find out what you really can do. And that courage will give you the freedom to fulfill your own potential to the greatest extent possible.

Throughout history, there are countless examples of people— even those who were very young—who exhibited uncommon courage in reaching their potential, often as it related to not only individual change but changes that impacted entire societies (and, in some cases, even the world). Joan of Arc was a mere peasant girl in medieval France when she decided God had chosen her to lead France to victory in the Hundred Years' War with England. With absolutely no military training, she led a French army to the blockaded city of Orléans, where the French secured a monumental victory over the English. Joan was captured, tried for witchcraft and heresy, and burned at the stake for her beliefs in 1431; she was only nineteen years old. In 1920 she was officially canonized, has long been considered one of history's greatest Saints, and remains a lasting symbol of French unity. Through her courage and grit, she changed her identity and became who she was meant to be.

Born into slavery in 1820 when she was twenty-nine years old, Harriet Tubman escaped to freedom in the North following the death of her owner. A sickly slave of low economic value, she feared for her safety and convinced her three brothers to escape with her from their Maryland plantation. But when the *Cambridge Democrat* ran a notice offering a $300 reward for return of the three brothers, the men went back to the plantation. But Harriet had no desire to remain in bondage. She saw a chance to change, and she set off alone for Pennsylvania.

Using the elaborate network of safe houses known as the Underground Railroad, Harriet traveled the ninety miles to Pennsylvania. As she crossed the border to freedom, she later recalled, "I looked at my hands to see if I was the same person. There was such a glory over everything; the sun came like gold through the trees, and over the fields, and I felt like I was in Heaven."[1]

---

1 "Harriet Tubman," Biography.com, https://www.biography.com/people/harriet-tubman-9511430.

Wanting to help others gain the freedom to act and think for themselves and become who they knew they could be, she became the most famous "conductor" on the Underground Railroad, risking her life to help hundreds of slaves escape bondage and gain their freedom. She also helped the Union Army during the Civil War, serving as a nurse, cook, scout, and armed spy. Following the war, she dedicated her life to helping impoverished former slaves.

The family of famous diarist Anne Frank suffered a different but no less dangerous kind of oppression.[2] Otto Frank and his family—which included his wife, Edith, and his two daughters, Margot and Anne—were among the many who tried and failed to escape Nazi persecution.

Frank first attempted to get visas to the United States for his family, but those efforts "ran afoul of restrictive American immigration policies designed to protect national security and guard against an influx of foreigners during time of war," wrote American University history professor Richard Breitman. What Breitman described as Frank's "tortuous process" of trying to gain freedom included sponsors, affidavits, large sums of money, and proof of how their entry would benefit America. "The moment the Franks and their American supporters overcame one administrative or logistical obstacle, another arose." But Frank never gave up trying. To him, freedom was everything.

---

2 Information about Anne Frank and her family taken from Elahe Izadi, "Anne Frank and Her Family Were Also Denied Entry as Refugees to the U.S.," *Washington Post*, November 24, 2015.

Restrictions were increasing, making it more and more difficult for foreigners—especially immigrants from Europe—to get into the United States. That's not all: the Nazis were making it increasingly more difficult to leave. By early 1939, there were more than three hundred thousand names on the waiting list for an immigration visa to the United States.

In 1941, after moving his family from Germany to the Netherlands, Frank again applied for visas to the United States. His applications were eventually destroyed. Frank pleaded with U.S. officials on April 30, 1941, writing, "Perhaps you remember that we have two girls. It is for the sake of the children mainly that we have to care for. Our own fate is of less importance."

Finally, on December 1, 1941, Frank paid the requisite $2,500 and got a Cuban visa for himself; he figured he would take things one day at a time and obtain freedom for his family as he could. Ten days later, Germany and Italy declared war on the United States. Frank's visa was canceled.

In 1942, the Frank family went into hiding in an attic apartment behind Frank's business in Amsterdam. It was the day after Margot Frank received a Nazi order to go to a labor camp and just a month after Anne Frank received a diary for her thirteenth birthday. That diary remains a classic work on the ability to maintain hope despite restricted freedom. After remaining in hiding for two years, everyone in the family was arrested on August 4, 1944. It is believed that someone betrayed them.

Otto Frank and his family were first deported to the Westerbork transit camp, then taken to Auschwitz. Otto was the only one to survive. His wife died of starvation, his girls of typhus. Anne was just fifteen years old when she died at the Bergen-Belsen concentration camp in Germany.

Yet another historical example of people who cherished and fought for the freedom to be who they envisioned is that of the pilgrims who came to the United States. Theirs was an issue of religious freedom: Devout Protestants from England, they had gone to Holland in an attempt to separate themselves from the Church of England and the Catholic Church—both of which they believed had strayed from the teachings of Jesus Christ and had established rituals that violated the teachings of the Bible. Striving for complete freedom to practice their religious beliefs, they courageously decided to set sail for America.

The pilgrims in Holland bought a small ship, the *Speedwell*, and sailed to Southampton to join English friends. The cargo ship, the *Mayflower*, would be making the journey alongside the *Speedwell*. The two ships set sail on August 15, 1620, but the *Speedwell* began leaking, and the group had to turn back twice. Of the original 120 passengers on the *Speedwell*, 102 stuffed themselves into the *Mayflower*, which was hastily refitted to accommodate passengers. The eighteen remaining passengers gave up in disgust and returned to England.

What was freedom worth to these intrepid souls? Imagine spending sixty-six days on the ocean with 120 people packed into a smelly cargo ship just ninety feet long (not even the length of half a football field). In October, North Atlantic high winds and heavy seas created ferocious conditions. A man who later served as governor of the Plymouth Colony wrote, "In many of these storms the winds were so fierce, and the seas so high, as they could not bear a knot of sail, but were forced to heave to, for many days together."

The *Mayflower* finally landed on November 9, 1620. Amazingly, only one passenger, a young servant named William Butten, died during the voyage. The rest of the freedom seekers climbed ashore on the other side of the Atlantic at what is now Massachusetts Bay.

Their troubles were scarcely over. They arrived so late they didn't have time to plant any crops, so they had no food. Though they had been promised financial support from friends in England, it never arrived. Starvation and sickness wiped out more than half of them, including eighteen of the thirty women of childbearing age. Those who did survive likely would have also perished had it not been for the generosity of the local Wampanoag Indians. Yet none of the pilgrims ever looked back; their privations were the sacrifice they were willing to make for freedom.

The people who have given up much for freedom—for the right to be, think, and act for themselves—are certainly not limited to those in the history books. There are many examples in our day of those who made tremendous sacrifices. Some who come immediately to mind include the military personnel defending the freedom of the United States (and their families); the police, firefighters, and citizens who rushed into the collapsing buildings to save lives on September 11, 2001; and the passengers aboard Flight 93 who rushed into the cockpit and prevented terrorists from attacking the United States Capitol and White House.

And there are others who have stood for freedom—not soldiers, not politicians, but ordinary people who made a choice for freedom in all its forms and who spoke up not only for themselves but for others who didn't have the courage to do so. Each one of us has the chance to be that person.

One of the most memorable remains anonymous to this day. On April 15, 1989, former Chinese Communist Party leader Hu Yaobang died; a man who had tried to move China toward a more open political system, he had become a symbol of democratic reform. Within three days, a mass protest began when thousands of mourning students marched through the streets of Beijing to Tiananmen Square. Ironically, the name *Tiananmen* means "gate of heavenly peace."

Things were anything but peaceful when thousands of citizens joined the students in the square to protest China's Communist rulers. By May 13, more than a hundred of the students in Tiananmen Square had begun a hunger strike; within a few days, the number participating in the strike swelled to several thousand.

By May 19, a rally at the square drew an estimated 1.2 million people. Desperate to put a stop to what he saw as a potential powder keg, Zhao Ziyang, general secretary of the Chinese Communist Party, addressed the rally and asked for an end to the demonstrations. That same day, Premier Li Peng imposed martial law.

By June 4, after several weeks of demonstrations, Chinese troops entered Tiananmen Square in several columns of tanks from the People's Liberation Army and began firing on students and civilians. An official death toll has never been released, but estimates range from several hundred to several thousand. An additional ten thousand or more were arrested. Several dozen were executed for their part in the demonstrations.

And that's when things got really interesting. On June 5, a column of tanks rumbled down Chang'an Avenue toward Tiananmen Square to suppress the protesters. At that moment, a single, unarmed man in a plain white shirt stepped out of the crowd and blocked the path of the tanks, persistently hindering their attempts to maneuver around him by continuing to step in their way. Just as it seemed the tanks would cut him down, a group of startled onlookers pulled the man back into the crowd, where he disappeared.

This solitary act of defiance was captured by photographer Stuart Franklin, whose picture became one of *Life* magazine's "100 Photos That Changed the World." Despite the fact that no one knows who he is, the "Unknown Rebel" was listed in *Time* as one of the hundred most influential people of the twentieth century. His defiant act was his way of fighting for the freedom of the Chinese people to change in myriad ways—to become what they wanted to become.

Another example with some similarities to Tiananmen Square is the incident in Saigon involving Thich Quang Duc, a devout Mahayana Buddhist monk who spent much of his life teaching, serving his people, leading monasteries, and rebuilding nearly thirty Buddhist temples. Well respected by his community, the seventy-six-year-old monk was chosen to carry out a stunning protest of the South Vietnamese government's oppressive policies.

The Buddhists in South Vietnam had been tyrannically persecuted to a point where they were no longer free to practice their religious beliefs. Thich Quang Duc could no longer tolerate the obstruction of freedom. On June 11, 1963, he sat in a full lotus position in the middle of a busy intersection in Saigon. There he loudly denounced government policies and called for religious equality for all people in South Vietnam.

When he finished his statement, horrified onlookers watched as his fellow monks doused his body with gasoline. Then Thich Quang Duc calmly set himself on fire, paying for his protest with his life.

While many disagreed with his method, no one could argue with its effectiveness. His suicide was a decisive turning point regarding the Buddhists in South Vietnam and ultimately led to a change in regime. In recognition of his selfless act of courage in defending freedom of thought, he has been deemed an enlightened being—and his heart, which is still intact, has become a holy relic.

Yet another man who fought for freedom—this time the freedom to follow the truth—did so in an atmosphere of war. First Lieutenant Ehren Watada was the first U.S. commissioned officer to refuse deployment to Iraq, and his action was based on what he believed to be false information being propagated by the military.

When he joined the army, Watada fully believed what the United States put forth as its justification for invading Iraq. But

after doing his own research, he concluded that the events leading to America's invasion of Iraq had been based on false evidence
presented to Congress. Perhaps the most disturbing to Watada was
what he believed to be false claims about Iraq possessing weapons
of mass destruction. As a result, Watada believed his involvement
in the invasion would constitute a crime against peace.

Watada had never been a quitter, and he didn't want to simply
leave the military. So he asked that his assignment be changed from
Iraq to Afghanistan—an area where he thought there was a true moral
imperative to defend the United States. The army refused his request
to be reassigned. In return, Watada refused to deploy to Iraq. When
the time came, he did not board the plane with the rest of his unit.

The army brought out the big guns in punishment. In February
2007, Watada was subjected to a court-martial—but the judge
declared a mistrial, saying Watada's claim of not following unlaw-
ful orders could not be determined in a military court. When a
second court-martial was ordered, Watada's attorney pointed out
that Watada could not be tried twice for the same charges.

For his "crime" of wanting freedom to speak the truth,
Watada—who now works at Fort Lewis in Durango, Colorado—
labors under the menacing threat of an eight-year prison term.

Although not involved in a military operation, Rosa Parks waged
war of a different kind. On December 1, 1955, forty-two-year-old
Parks boarded the Cleveland Avenue bus in Montgomery, Alabama,
headed home after a long day's work as a seamstress. She took a seat

in the first of several rows designated for "colored" passengers, as was required by law on the city's segregated buses.

All public transportation in Alabama was segregated at the time, a line roughly in the middle of the bus demarcating the seats for white passengers (in the front) and black passengers (in the back). A black passenger was required to get on through the front door of the bus, pay the fare, get off the bus again, and reboard through the back door. All city bus drivers were given the powers of a city police officer while operating the bus.

As the bus continued on its route that day, it started to fill up with white passengers. The bus driver noticed that several white passengers were standing in the aisle, so he stopped the bus, moved the sign separating the two sections back one row, and asked four black passengers, including Parks, to give up their seats so the white passengers could sit down. It wasn't an uncommon practice—and bus drivers could call the police to remove any black passengers who refused to give up their seats.

The other three black passengers quickly gave up their seats. But Rosa Parks didn't budge. When the bus driver demanded she stand up, she calmly replied, "I don't think I should have to stand up." The bus driver called the police, who arrested Parks and took her to police headquarters. She was released on bail later that night.

When she arrived at court the next morning for sentencing, a crowd of more than five hundred supporters cheered her on. Found guilty of violating a local ordinance, she was given what amounted to a brisk slap on the hand: a ten-dollar fine accompanied by a four-dollar administrative fee. The *real* story of the morning was what happened as a result of her arrest and trial.

What came to be known as the Montgomery Bus Boycott lasted 381 days. The city's African-American residents refused to ride the buses, which were virtually empty; instead, some carpooled or rode cabs operated by African-Americans. But most of the city's estimated forty thousand African-Americans chose to walk to work in protest, some marching as far as twenty miles rather than ride the bus. Dozens of buses sat idle throughout the boycott, severely compromising the city's transit-services budget.

Retaliation was swift. The city canceled the insurance on taxis driven by African-Americans. Black churches were burned. Martin Luther King Jr.'s house was bombed. A number of black citizens were arrested for violating an obsolete law against boycotts. In the end, though, the city of Montgomery had no choice but to lift the law requiring segregation on city buses. The quiet refusal of Rosa Parks to vacate her seat ultimately launched a nationwide effort to end the segregation of all public facilities, not just buses.

Even though she became a symbol of the nation's Civil Rights movement, Rosa Parks suffered as a result of having had the courage to stand for freedom. In the months following the boycott, she lost her seamstress job at a Montgomery department store; her husband was also fired from his job after his boss banned him from talking about his wife or their legal case. Neither was able to find other work in Montgomery. Finally, Rosa, her husband, and her mother moved to Detroit, Michigan, where she secured a job as a receptionist and secretary in the office of U.S. representative John Conyers.

Rosa Parks, Ehren Watada, Thich Quang Duc, and the "Unnamed Rebel" at Tiananmen Square were all fighting for the same thing: freedom of choice. So were Joan of Arc, Harriet Tubman, Otto Frank, and the pilgrims. When you are trying to reinvent adversity, one of the most critical kinds of emancipation you can have is freedom of choice—the ability to choose from at least two available options *without being constrained* by someone or something else.

We often associate confinement with prison—inmates locked up, unable to leave the confines of their cell blocks. They are told what they can eat. What they can do. How they can interact with others. Every facet of their lives, in fact, is restricted by those tasked with keeping them in order.

No one wants that sort of constraint. But too often—especially in the throes of adversity—it is possible to put those kinds of limits on yourself. It is possible that the way you think about yourself, the way you identify yourself, and the beliefs you have about your potential and future confine you just as much as if you were incarcerated behind bars. If you have given up on yourself, you might as well be enslaved because you have limited your own options.

Right now, in the middle of the adversity howling around your ears, how do you identify yourself? Is it by what you do for a living? The clothes you wear? The house you live in? The car you drive? The amount of money in your bank account? The balance on your credit cards? The way you are treated by others? The fact that you have not achieved your dreams?

This minute, as you are trying to climb out of the abyss of adversity, do you feel limited by regrets? By resentment? By a feeling of hopelessness that squeezes the very life out of you? Then you are, in a very real sense, in prison, just as much as if you were clad in an orange jumpsuit and assigned a number. But here's the good news: even if all these things exist right now, you have the opportunity to get out of that prison—without doing any more time and without having to answer to anyone else.

Here's why: every minute of every day, you have the freedom—yes, freedom—to choose how you look at things and how you will respond to what life is dishing up. No one can ever take that freedom away from you. It is a God-given right that is yours for the taking.

No discussion of emotional emancipation—the freedom to become whatever you want to be—would be complete without looking at Viktor Frankl. Born in Vienna to a Jewish family of civil servants, he developed an early interest in psychology and eventually studied medicine at the University of Vienna, where he specialized in neurology and psychiatry. He focused his studies on depression and suicide.

When the Nazi regime caught up with him on September 25, 1942, Frankl, his wife, Tilly, and his parents, Gabriel and Elsa, were deported to the Nazi Theresienstadt ghetto. There, he was assigned to work in a clinic, and when his specific skills were noticed, he was assigned to a psychiatric ward and tasked with providing mental health care. Frankl capitalized on his specialized areas of study by setting up a unit to help newcomers overcome shock and grief. Later, he and another doctor at the ghetto organized a suicide watch. He also gave a series of open lectures on all aspects of staying mentally healthy even in dire circumstances.

While at Theresienstadt, his father, Gabriel, died of pneumonia and pulmonary edema. On October 19, 1944, Frankl and his wife were transported to the Auschwitz concentration camp. It was the first in a series of moves for Frankl: just six days later he was moved to a camp affiliated with Dachau, where he spent five months in slave labor. In March 1945, he was moved to Türkheim, where he worked as a physician. Soon after, on April 27, 1945, the camp was liberated by American soldiers.

Frankl's mother and brother, Walter, died at Auschwitz. He was separated from his wife when she was moved to Bergen-Belsen, where she died. The only other survivor of the Nazi regime in Frankl's immediate family was his sister, Stella, who had emigrated to Australia.

After three grueling years in the camps, you would think Frankl was a broken man. But he returned to Vienna determined to find a sense of meaning that would enable him to overcome his painful experiences while in captivity. The result of that work is his now internationally famous book, *Man's Search for Meaning*.[3]

In this landmark publication, Frankl pointed out that "between stimulus and response there is a space. In that space is our power to

---

3 Viktor E. Frankl, *Man's Search for Meaning* (originally published in 1946; Boston, MA: Beacon Press, 1959, 1962, 1984, 1992, and 2006).

choose our response. In our response lies our growth and our free-dom." In other words, whenever *anything* happens to you, there is a period of time during which you choose how you will respond. In that period of time—whether it be seconds, minutes, days, or even longer—you are *empowered. You* decide what your response will be. *You* decide how you will react. With your response, *you* determine how you will grow. And therein, says Frankl, is your freedom.

Perhaps Frankl's greatest gift to each of us is the meaning behind his best-known statement: "Everything can be taken from a man but one thing: the last of the human freedoms—to choose one's attitude in any given set of circumstances, to choose one's own way."

No matter what happens to you—no matter what kind of adversity is slamming you against the corners of life—no one can take away your freedom to choose your attitude in your particular set of circumstances, to choose your own way. That is always and forever yours, and it determines whether you thrive and reinvent your adversity into an opportunity for great achievement.

Another of Frankl's quotes, this one far less known, also holds great significance if you're battling adversity: "When we are no longer able to change a situation, we are challenged to change our-selves." And here's the glorious news about that: you may *never* be able to change your circumstances, but you will *always* be able to change yourself. *You* have the freedom to make that change, and *you* have the freedom to start right now.

Here's what else that means: no matter your circumstances, you can choose to be happy. Grateful. Hopeful. You can choose to have dignity of spirit and freedom of soul, even when everything about you seems to be crumbling around your ears. You can choose emotional emancipation.

You have so much freedom in your circumstance, no matter what that circumstance is, even if you can't see freedom at first glance. But it's there. You are free to give up resentment. You are free to let go of misery. You are free to banish sadness. You are free to reject anger. You are free to move beyond agony to achievement regardless of your circumstance. I love the sage words of the Buddha. I think they apply to all kinds of negative emotions: "Holding on to anger is like grasping a hot coal with the intent of throwing it at someone else; you are the one who gets burned." You have the freedom, starting right now, to make sure you don't get burned. Not ever again.

Best of all, you have the freedom to believe in yourself. During the storms of adversity, it's easy to give up on yourself. It seems everything is conspiring against you and it's all you can do to stay vertical some days. I get that. I've been there. But through it all—through all the pain and suffering, trials and tribulations, devastation and betrayal, and heartache and difficulty—shines your magnificent spirit, that compelling life force that determines your ability to overcome every obstacle and emerge victorious at the end of every battle. Never, ever give up on yourself.

Right now you have a choice: you can become whoever you want to become. It doesn't depend on your bank account or whether you're married or how your friends treat you or the fact that you got passed over for a promotion at work. *The choice is yours.* Until you realize this with all of your being, you have surrendered your most valuable possession: your freedom to choose.

So please *choose*. Choose life and happiness and achievement. Choose to make the very most out of what you've been given. Choose to turn your back on the naysayers and the obstacles and the disappointments and the adversity. Choose to embrace the time you have, and choose to make the most of it. Countless people have died for the right to choose; don't die before you realize *you have a choice.*

You were born for a reason. It's time you discover that reason and let others know what it is. If you're not in a place where you can fulfill that reason, move to a different place. Walk away from the people holding you back, and surround yourself with those who support you and want the best for you. Your life can change dramatically *if you are willing to make the change.* You can choose who you will become, and that is the ultimate freedom.

Adopt and embrace my seven-step freedom acronym, which will enable you to rise beyond the ashes, reinvent yourself, and move from agony to achievement:

Forgive—forgive yourself and others. Realize your part in the adversity.

Rejuvenate, Replenish, and Reward yourself—make time for you.

Embrace your possibility—change your perception, change your life.

Express gratitude while being enlightened—be thankful for your growth; there is no growth without adversity.

Don't quit; stay in the game—your chance of winning is based on your commitment to stay the course. Quittin' is simply not an option!

Own your fear—take ownership of the fear as opposed to allowing fear to own you. Owning fear is simply taking a stand to fear no more

Move beyond agony to achievement—your time is now.

In her epic work *Jane Eyre*, Charlotte Brontë wrote, "I am no bird; and no net ensnares me: I am a free human being with an independent will." You too are free of any restraint, of anything designed by man or nature to hold you back. You have the choice, and you can achieve the emotional emancipation that will allow you to reinvent any adversity you face, now or in the future.

Choose. Soar. Become.

Grab the opportunity to be what you never thought you could be. It is well within reach.

Chapter Two

Facing Adversity with Grace and Courage

*[He] who accepts a trial as an invitation to grow can
find peace in the midst of the struggle.*

—*Henry B. Eyring*

Whoever we are, whatever our station in life, we have one thing in common: we must all deal with adversity. No one escapes. No one lives an existence of perpetual ease and comfort.

And that's the way it was designed by a God who loves us as His children and cares about our well-being. If that seems difficult to believe, please keep reading.

Adversity, according to Webster's dictionary, is "an adverse or unfavorable fortune or fate; a condition marked by misfortune, calamity, or distress." It's a state of persistent misfortune, difficulty, tragedy, or hard times. (That *still* may not sound like something a loving God wants or allows, but please trust me here.)

One word in that definition is particularly important: *persistent.* Adversity isn't a temporary or one-time hardship, like breaking a heel right before an important business meeting. Instead, it's not having any shoes at all.

Adversity isn't going for two weeks without a call from your child who attends college in a distant state. Instead, it's having your child's face plastered all over posters nailed to phone poles because no one has seen her since Christmas.

Adversity isn't burning dinner minutes before important guests are scheduled to arrive; it's having the house and everything in it burn to the ground because the wind fueled the flames from the barbecue grill on the patio. Oh, and losing your two toddlers because they couldn't get out quickly enough.

That's adversity.

Breaking a heel or missing a phone call or burning dinner don't require grace or courage. Not really—not in the long run, anyway. They happen, then they're over. You may feel temporary embarrassment or frustration, but then you move on. But facing winter with no shoes or burying a child or finding yourself homeless after a devastating fire all require you to dig into the deepest places of your soul for the sheer valor to keep on going. Real adversity—the kind that tears at your heart and leaves you reeling—calls for real courage.

And sooner or later, if you haven't already, you're going to need it.

Maybe you're not going through any particular adversity right now, and maybe you're tempted to skip this chapter. If that's what you think, please think again. Don't get complacent just because you currently have the bull by the horns and are working the game! Life has a way of surprising everyone with the curveball of adversity when it's least expected. You never know when the next curveball is heading for you, so use the information I'm about to share to help you prepare to renew, revive, and grow to your next level.

Because sooner or later—and sometimes during many different times in your life—comfort will give way to distress. Good health will be threatened by chronic illness. Misfortune will come knocking at your door. And if you've been enjoying relative peace and comfort, especially for quite a while, you may find yourself afraid or even angry when adversity interrupts your life. You may *especially* feel that way if it seems you've already had more than your share and it doesn't seem you can catch a break. You may find yourself asking the question so many ask when faced with the sting of adversity: *Why me?*

It's a question and a situation that can cause you to doubt your mettle. Can cause your spirits to fade. Can leave you questioning whether the love of God (or anyone else) is enough to pull you through—or, for that matter, whether God loves you at all. If adversity becomes severe enough or prolonged enough or is repeated enough, it may even leave you questioning if there *is* a God.

That's certainly one way of responding to adversity. But there is another, arguably better way—one that will help you discover a purpose that enables you to face whatever arises with strength and determination. Best of all, responding to adversity in a healthy way helps you pull out of it so you can move on and fashion a new life filled with impossibly good things.

Where does adversity come from, anyway? Sometimes it results from our own poor choices or mistakes. For example, you may be burdened fielding calls from bill collectors and struggling to make ends meet because you bought too many things on credit instead of waiting until you could pay cash.

Adversity can also result from the bad choices of others. I experienced cataclysmic adversity because my CFO ran two sets of books and misappropriated money in my company. You may undergo incredible pain when your child dies from a drug overdose. Your spouse's infidelity may result in the eventual breakup of your marriage. You may suffer abuse at the hands of another.

Sometimes adversity comes merely because we are mortals with bodies that become ill, get injured, or age—and we are generally not able to control disease, accidental injury, or the ravages of time.

Whatever its origin, we know that adversity is not new; it is, in fact, as old as time itself. There are numerous examples in scripture of people who faced tremendous adversity. Imagine how Eve felt when one of her sons killed his brother. In the midst of prolonged and constant persecution, Jeremiah was lowered into a cistern with ropes and left to languish in the mud. Even after being anointed king, David was relentlessly chased by Saul, who vowed to take his life. The Apostle Paul suffered persecution, imprisonment, and prolonged separation from those he loved; he also referred to a never-ending "thorn in the flesh" that kept him from being exalted (2 Corinthians 12:7).

And then there is the scriptural poster person for adversity: Job. The Bible tells us he "was perfect and upright, and one that feared God, and eschewed evil" (Job 1:1). Certainly he of all men would be blessed, protected from trial. Not so. A wealthy man, he lost all his possessions and property. Then *all* his children died. Then he was covered with boils and suffered tremendous physical pain. His wife, overcome with sorrow, told him to simply give up—to curse God and die. When three of his friends finally showed up to comfort him, they instead maintained he must have committed some dastardly sin to deserve such punishment.

Not really the kind of "comfort" one would seek under the circumstances.

Adversity hasn't afflicted only those in the scriptures; countless people throughout history have fought incredible hardship. Some are famous; some you've never heard of. Some may be in your own family or live in your neighborhood. *You* may be one.

Try these on for size. Stephen Hawking has one of the most brilliant scientific minds in the world but was diagnosed at the age of twenty-one with amyotrophic lateral sclerosis (ALS), or Lou Gehrig's disease. Almost completely paralyzed, he has spent most of his life in a wheelchair, helpless to take care of his most basic needs; he can communicate only through a device that generates speech for him. Yet his work in the field of physics and cosmology can be described as nothing other than groundbreaking, and his best-selling *A Brief History of Time*—only one of the dozen or more books he has written—has unlocked some of the world's greatest physical mysteries.

Performing live on the piano and violin by the time he was seven, legendary composer Ludwig van Beethoven went almost completely deaf after starting to lose his hearing at the age of twenty-six. Though he couldn't hear his own music, he went on to compose nine symphonies, thirty-two piano sonatas, five piano concertos, one opera, and a number of chamber works and pieces for string quartets.

Franklin Delano Roosevelt served four terms as president of the United States despite being paralyzed from the waist down by the polio virus, which he contracted when thirty-six. Refusing to admit he was disabled, he opened a treatment center for other polio victims at Warm Springs, Georgia, where patients received cutting-edge treatment. That's not all: he brought the nation out of the Great Depression, instituted the New Deal, and led the United States to victory in World War II before dying during his fourth term in office.

Profoundly deaf and blind from an illness that struck when she was only nineteen months old, Helen Keller's stubborn determination and being blessed with a gifted teacher enabled her to learn how to communicate with others. She wrote a short story at age eleven, penned her autobiography at age twenty-two, and became an exceptional activist for women's suffrage and labor rights.

The list goes on, both of the famous and the obscure. Prolific author Charles Dickens suffered with debilitating epilepsy from the time he was a young child. Popular actor Michael J. Fox was stricken with Parkinson's disease and became an outspoken advocate for finding a cure. Brilliant musician Stevie Wonder was born six weeks early and suffered detached retinas, leading to lifelong, incurable blindness—yet had his first number-one hit at the age of three.

At the age of thirteen, Bethany Hamilton lost her arm in a shark attack—along with half her blood—but went on to win a number of surfing competitions. First Lieutenant Melissa Stockwell lost one of her legs to a roadside bomb in Baghdad, earning both a Bronze Star and the Purple Heart; she has dedicated her energies since then to helping other amputees. She is a consistent medal-winner in the Paralympics, where she competes in running, biking, and swimming and is a two-time world champion in the paratriathlon.

And here's a particularly poignant example of overcoming adversity: seven-year-old Pennsylvania first grader Annie Clark recently won $1,000 and a trophy in a penmanship contest—despite the fact that she was born without hands. She writes by lodging a pencil between her arms. And that's not all: she also paints and colors using the same technique.

Let's go back to the scriptures for a minute, because several of Christ's Apostles recommended a surprising response to adversity. James wrote, "My brethren, *count it all joy* when ye fall into divers temptations; knowing this, that the trying of your faith worketh patience. But let patience have her perfect work, that ye may be perfect and entire, wanting nothing" (James 1:2–4; emphasis added). "Count it all joy." Not a typical response to gut-wrenching calamity.

While the natural tendency is to dread any prolonged trial, Paul wrote in his epistle to the Romans, "*We glory in tribulations* also: knowing that tribulation worketh patience, and patience, experience; and experience, hope. . . . For when we were yet without strength, in due time Christ died for the ungodly" (Romans 5:3–6; emphasis added). There's that *patience* concept again. It seems they may be on to something.

Summing up his epistle to Timothy, the Apostle Paul wrote more about the best way to deal with adversity and the blessing such a response can bring: "For I am now ready to be offered, and the time of my departure is at hand. *I have fought a good fight, I have finished my course, I have kept the faith*: Henceforth there is laid up for me a crown of righteousness, which the Lord, the righteous judge, shall give me at that day: *and not to me only*, but unto all them also that love his appearing" (2 Timothy 4:5–8; emphasis added).

The message is clear: *all* who fight a good fight, who finish the course, who keep the faith—in other words, all who face adversity with grace and courage, nothing wavering—can lay claim to a remarkable reward. And here's the best part: we aren't required to wait until we reach the shores of heaven to claim that reward. It is here for us now and will give us strength for the journey today.

And something we need to understand right up front about adversity is that it is *not the end*. Yes, it is hard. It's supposed to be. Yes, it may take us to the limits of our endurance. It's supposed to do that, too. But the Apostle Paul, who was well acquainted with adversity, gives us a tremendous perspective on it: "We are troubled on every side, yet not distressed; we are perplexed, but not in despair; persecuted, but not forsaken; cast down, but not destroyed; . . . though our outward man perish, yet the inward man is renewed day by day" (2 Corinthians 4:8, 16). Did you hear that? Even though it seems we'll never make it, we will actually be renewed *day by day.* That's the promise and the possibility of adversity. And it all depends on how we respond to it.

The way we respond to adversity has a great influence on whether it becomes a roadblock and obstacle or a superhighway to learning and growth. When we hang on to adversity and anguish over it for all we're worth, it drags us down. When we face it and acknowledge it as a vehicle to eventual happiness and progress, the adversity becomes an entirely different experience. Simply stated, "Change your perception, change your life."

It's easy to get derailed by adversity. You have probably known someone who has responded to suffering—*especially* when it was someone else's fault—with resentment, anger, bitterness, doubt, or fear. Maybe you've felt those things yourself when your life has been thrown into chaos by circumstances you couldn't control. (You may have even felt that way if the problems were partially your fault.) But when you consider all the reasons why adversity blesses you, it is much easier to respond with faith, patience, and hope born of that "peace . . . which passeth all understanding" (Philippians 4:6–7).

So before we consider the best ways to respond to adversity, let's look at the *purpose* of adversity—why a God who loves us sometimes allows us to suffer through things that are so scathingly difficult.[4] And why something so hard is, in the end, actually good for us.

In speaking of adversity, Orson F. Whitney—a politician, journalist, poet, historian, and academic—explained, "No pain that we suffer, no trial that we experience is wasted. It ministers to our education, to the development of such qualities as patience, faith, fortitude, and humility. All that we suffer and all that we endure, especially when we endure it patiently, builds up our characters, purifies our hearts, expands our souls, and makes us more tender and charitable." When we truly understand the purpose of adversity, we come to realize there is no waste in what happens as a result.

Adversity Gets Your Attention

Few things get your attention like adversity. Once something really difficult shows up, it's no longer possible to just keep going along in the same way, along the same path, doing the same thing. You have to stop—sometimes very abruptly—and take a critical look at what's happening. You have to marshal all your abilities and figure out what you're going to do *now*. And one thing is certain: you will need to change some things about how you are "doing life."

That may sound bad on the surface, but think about it: being forced to face problems and find solutions constitutes an incredible teacher that offers better, more effective lessons than just about

---

4 Some of the information on the purposes of adversity is adapted from the Institute in Basic Life Principles *Training Faithful Men Resource Manual* (Oak Brook, IL: IBLP Publications, 1984), 33–37.

anything else. In that process, you will likely land on some new ways of approaching your situation that end up making you stronger, better, smarter, and happier.

There's nothing like getting out of a rut, and there's nothing like adversity to make that happen.

Adversity Demands Self-Examination

Once you've experienced the need to abruptly abandon your usual casual routine, something else happens as a result of adversity: you are forced to examine yourself. What you're doing. How you're handling things. What you may be able to do under these new circumstances.

When things are going well, you're just not motivated to deeply examine yourself. It takes effort, and it's easy to put off—for a good, long time. But when adversity enters the scene, it's the only smart way to approach things. Getting a solid idea of where you are, where you want to be, and how to get there is the first step in handling the challenge of adversity.

Adversity Challenges You to Reevaluate Your Priorities

Reevaluating your priorities allows you to figure out what is most important at any given time—and helps you figure out where you should be putting the bulk of your attention, energy, and time.

And that's especially important when you're dealing with adversity, which tends to make *everything* seem urgent.

When everything seems urgent, everything loses its urgency. When everything seems important, suddenly nothing is most important. You find yourself spinning your wheels, needlessly shifting your gears, and wasting a whole lot of time and energy just trying to figure out what to do next. In those cases, sadly, often *nothing* gets done and you end up feeling more overwhelmed and out of control than ever.

If adversity has shoved more onto your plate than you think you can reasonably handle, it's more critical than ever to size things up and determine what should take priority. Identifying the things that are most important enables you to work on those things first, which can go a long way toward empowering you.

Adversity Exposes Your Weaknesses

Oh, great, you may be thinking, *just what I need—the world as I know it is caving in on me, and now I need to face up to my weaknesses? Good times.*

Believe it or not, it *is* good times. And here's why: until you acknowledge a weakness, you'll never succeed at overcoming it— converting it to a strength. The Apostle Paul captured the essence of that principle when he wrote, "I take pleasure in infirmities, in reproaches, in necessities, in persecutions, in distresses . . . for when I am weak, then am I strong" (2 Corinthians 12:10).

Becoming strong where you are now weak is one of the keys to moving forward with a purpose. That means you need to know where you are weak—and adversity helps you see that better than almost anything else.

Adversity also brings out the best in us, because when we are embroiled in the most difficult battles, we learn what it is we are made of. Maya Angelou sums it up nicely: "You may encounter many defeats, but you must not be defeated. In fact, it may be necessary to encounter the defeats, so you can know who you are, what you can rise from, how you can still come out of it."

Adversity Grooms Us to Help Others

One of the most valuable purposes of adversity is that it prepares you to comfort and serve others. Having gone through your own harrowing hardship, you become uniquely qualified to help and serve and bless someone else going through their own daunting experience. Here's a simplistic way of illustrating this: if you are diagnosed with breast cancer, who do you turn to for help and understanding? That's right—someone who went through and survived breast cancer. No one can identify with others like those who have experienced the same pain.

But know this, too: the very act of being pushed to the limit brings with it universal experiences that can then give you the wisdom to help someone who is suffering, with just about anything. You can share ways to develop patience, endurance, reliance. You can offer comfort born of your own adversity. You can just *be there*. The details don't matter; the sharing and concern and genuine care do.

Adversity Prepares You for Greater Things

Helen Keller, who had every right to be bitter and angry over her profound disabilities, wrote, "I thank God for my handicaps, for through them, I have found myself, my work, and my God."

Turning once again to the scriptures, we see numerous examples of people put through the fire of adversity as a way of preparing them for greater purposes. Let's look at just one: Joseph of Egypt.

Joseph learned the sting of adversity early in life, and he had to have realized that his life was anything but "normal." If anyone in the Bible had a right to ask "Why me?" it was Joseph. His brothers, tasked with protecting him, threw him into a pit instead and left him there to die, stripping him of the coat his father had given him. He spent years in prison without cause. Later, he was sold into slavery. He was troubled by unusual and disturbing dreams.

Before it was all over, he found himself second in command to powerful Pharaoh. You see, Joseph had been prepared for a glorious purpose; the adversity he suffered refined his character and prepared him to fulfill that purpose. He saved from starvation not only the brothers who tossed him into the pit but an entire nation. Through all the travail Joseph suffered, God had a plan in mind. Joseph didn't know what that plan was, but God did.

As you endure your adversity, it's certain God has a plan for you. You may not know what that plan is, but God does. Your job is to trust Him.

Adversity Lets You Be Tested

Religious leader and scholar Neal A. Maxwell once wisely said, "How can you and I really expect to glide naively through life, as if to say, 'Lord, give me experience, but not grief, not sorrow, not pain, not opposition, not betrayal, and certainly not be forsaken.'" It is as though we are asking the Lord to keep from us all the experiences that made the Lord what He is—yet in the same breath asking Him to let us share in His joy.[5]

That will never happen.

All of written history testifies to the way in which people have been tested by adversity. Scripture certainly does. The children of Israel tramped through the wilderness for *forty years*—much of it, unbeknownst to them, going around in circles—before they were allowed to reach the promised land. The Lord Himself said they were tested "to humble [them] and to test [them] in order to know what was in [their] heart" (Exodus 16:4). Job was tested as God allowed Satan to bring one affliction after another upon him; he was scarcely allowed to catch his breath before the next thing happened. But no matter what Satan heaped on Job, the Lord observed that Job "still maintained his integrity, though you incited me

---

5 Neal A. Maxwell, "Lest Ye Be Wearied and Faint in Your Minds," *Ensign*, May 1991, 88.

against him to ruin him without any reason" (Job 2:3). The Lord knew, and Satan knew, and Job himself knew where his loyalties lay. He passed the test with flying colors.

Each of us is tested in different ways. The test *you* receive is designed to develop something specific in you. It is for your good. And as you press forward through the adversity, you will realize what that is. The Apostle James put it this way: "Blessed is the man who perseveres under trial, because when he has stood the test, he will receive the crown of life that God has promised to those who love him" (James 1:12).

Adversity Drives You to Your Knees

When adversity comes with all its distress, sometimes you simply can't make it on your own. At these times, you are driven to your knees for help from a divine source—and you will likely be prompted to cry out to God, who watches over all His children. And it is then, as the Psalmist promises, "The righteous cry, and the Lord heareth, and delivereth them out of all their troubles" (Psalms 34:17).

What if it seems God doesn't hear right away? What if, despite your crying, the adversity continues—maybe even worsens? It doesn't mean God has turned a deaf ear. It means you still have much to learn, much to experience, much more time to spend petitioning Him for help. In all that petitioning, your soul *will* be comforted, even if the circumstances surrounding you do not ease up. You will learn with great clarity how the Lord is able to ease the burdens on your back even while you yet bear them.

Ask yourself this: If you can't trust God in the tough times, when *can* you trust Him? We learn through adversity that we can trust Him at all times—even in the most difficult ones. We must all experience grace to know that it really exists, and the *only* way to experience it is to have to rely on it. And the most certain way to rely on it is to be driven to our knees in a circumstance in which we have only that grace and only the tiniest shreds of our own strength left.

How to Face and Transform Adversity

Nobody *wants* to face adversity, but it *will* happen—and, handled in a positive and healthy way, you won't just survive, you'll grow, evolve, and thrive. Instead of allowing adversity to define who you are, you can face adversity with courage, strength, faith, and patience that will transform your life and show you the meaning of God's grace.

I am sharing the best ways to face adversity because my frequent experiences with adversity have schooled me and altered my life. I had an alcoholic and abusive father, something that caused me to look for love in all the wrong places; after four failed marriages, I am still single. I grew up in grinding poverty, suffering all the hardships that come along with it. I developed an autoimmune disease that brought with it one serious health issue after another. Most recently, I lost everything I had because of the decisions of my company's CFO—something that took me to the edge and helped me understand why some people are driven to take their own lives.

As I attended the classroom of adversity in each of these situations, though, I was able to find purpose and meaning in what they brought to my life. And looking back on all of them (as well as anticipating those yet to come), I now recognize them as gifts, teaching me things I could have learned in no other way.

That's the background I bring. That's what I have to offer. And I offer it to you in the prayer that you will recognize in your adversity the same opportunities I found.

Showing Courage in the Face of Adversity

Courage has been defined as the ability to do something that frightens you—to demonstrate strength in the face of pain. And if there's anything that can frighten you, it is adversity. When it first strikes in all its fury, it can literally knock the wind out of you; as it continues, maybe for years, adversity can sometimes require all the courage you have just to face another day.

But courage is one of the most important traits needed to face and transform adversity. I have always loved what Nelson Mandela had to say about his ordeal: "I learned that courage was not the absence of fear, but the triumph over it. The brave man is not he who does not feel afraid, but he who conquers that fear."

Yes. You may feel afraid. You may feel *very* afraid. But the good news is that you can draw on courage to triumph over not only your fear but over adversity itself.

My purpose here is *not* to give you a primer on courage; I'm betting you know all about it, because I'm betting you've had to draw on courage many times in your life. I'm also betting you've seen examples of it all around you. My purpose here *is* to show you a few examples of people who have demonstrated uncommon courage so you can benefit from those examples and take inspiration for your own life.

One of the most stirring I know of is Pakistani teen Malala Yousafzai, winner of the Liberty Medal (awarded each year to a person of courage and conviction) and, at seventeen, the youngest person ever to be awarded the Nobel Peace Prize. She was celebrated for her resilience and courage in the face of adversity—after almost being killed as she stood up for a child's right to get an education.

At the tender age of eleven, she started authoring a blog for the BBC under a pen name. In it, she documented her life as a schoolgirl under Taliban rule in the Swat Valley of northern Pakistan. When the Taliban subsequently banned education for girls in the region, Malala couldn't restrain herself. Her voice grew louder, and she became a target. The Taliban vowed to silence her.

In 2012, Malala was on a bus traveling home from school when a Taliban gunman raided the bus and shot her in the head, intending to kill her. The bullet went through her head and into her neck before exiting through her shoulder. I'm guessing she was horrifically afraid as she stared down the barrel of that gun, but she never backed down. Through a miracle of God, she did not die on that bus. She was taken to an English hospital, where—through sheer grit and determination, and, of course, the grace of God—she recovered from her wounds.

But that wasn't the end of Malala or her astonishing determination. She went on to co-found the Malala Fund, an organization that advocates for equal rights to an education for all children regardless of circumstance. She donated her $100,000 in prize money from the Liberty Medal to Pakistani children in need.

Philadelphia mayor Michael A. Nutter, who presided at the ceremony where Malala received the Liberty Medal observed, "Malala shows you don't even have to be of voting age to let your voice be heard."

Another speaker at the ceremony—Minnijean Brown-Trickey, one of the "Little Rock Nine" African-American students who fought for the right to attend a segregated Arkansas high school in 1957, said, "Why does any ordinary person do something extraordinary? We do it because someone has to do it." Her words bring with it remarkable vision: as you face adversity with courage, you become the ordinary person who does something extraordinary.

Malala Yousafzai is a remarkable example of courage in the face of adversity, but she is only one example. Developing and maintaining courage through adversity is a journey that will be different for every person who undertakes it, and there are many who demonstrate dignity and perseverance as they face incredible odds. Let's look at a few more.

Famed Greek philosopher Socrates stuck to his revolutionary opinions and beliefs rather than cave in to those who persecuted him for doing so. Arrested for his teachings, he refused to back down. He was calm in the face of adversity and willing to die for his beliefs, which he was ultimately forced to do.

Dietrich Bonhoeffer, a Lutheran pastor in Germany, was persecuted by a Nazi regime that tried to keep him from preaching the things he knew to be true. Instead of retreating in silence, abandoning his efforts to teach what he considered to be the word of God, or even fleeing for his life, he chose to stay in the land of his birth and fulfill his calling. Maintaining his courage to the end, he was arrested and executed in the Flossian concentration camp.

Another who demonstrated great courage in similar adversity was Witold Pilecki, who suspected unspeakable atrocities were taking place behind closed doors. In 1943, he volunteered to smuggle himself into the Auschwitz concentration camp—a place so many were trying to escape!—so he could report to the Allies what was really happening there. He was able to later break away and played an instrumental role in the Warsaw uprising of 1944. Four years later, the Stalinist secret police executed him for staying loyal to the non-Communist government in Poland.

In 1940, Britain stood alone in its opposition to Nazi Germany. Many in the country's leadership wanted to seek a deal with Hitler, convinced it would help protect the nation against attack. But Winston Churchill faced the adversity of such a possible outcome with courage and determination, voicing his intention to fight on. In the end, his resolution and valor inspired the entire nation through its darkest hour, resulting in an Allied victory over the threat of domination.

Nelson Mandela braved incredible adversity in his fight to end the unjust system of apartheid in South Africa. Jailed for his political beliefs, he was sentenced to twenty years in prison—an almost unheard-of penalty. Refusing to back down from his beliefs, he spent those twenty years in punitive hard labor, separated from the people and things he loved. Upon his release, he was elected to lead a free South Africa.

Refusing to vacate her seat on that bus on December 1, 1955, Rosa Parks had long suffered the prolonged adversity of oppression and racial discrimination—and she was done. Rather than bow to the demand to move, she allowed herself to be dragged from the bus and was physically attacked before being arrested for refusing to give up her seat to a white passenger. Her single act of bravery, a feat of nonviolent resistance, led to desegregation of all city buses.

Another leader in the struggle for racial equality, Martin Luther King, faced incredible adversity throughout his mission: he was arrested more than twenty times for taking part in nonviolent protests. He received almost constant threatening phone calls. He was violently attacked on multiple occasions, even being stabbed in one of the assaults. His home was bombed and set on fire. And he paid the ultimate price—that of his life. But his courage in adversity inspired a nation and resulted in landmark civil-rights legislation.

Clearly the greatest example of courage in the face of adversity was Jesus Christ, who stuck to the truth of His message regardless of the consequences, which were often harrowing. There were many times He could have changed His message and escaped the torture, pain, and humiliation inflicted by those determined to silence Him. In the greatest story ever told, He gave His life blood for the cause of truth and His commitment to His mission.

Showing Strength in the Face of Adversity

The concept of strength encompasses a number of traits. Often associated only with physical prowess or capacity, strength is also a *feeling* of power. It's accepting who you are and loving yourself. It's keeping your commitments no matter what others say or do. It's facing your fears. It's being brave and taking risks. It's being truthful with yourself and those around you.

And it's a key to facing and transforming adversity and making of it a positive experience from which you can learn and grow. Gathering your strength in the face of adversity is what will help you be your best and reach your potential regardless of the fury pounding against your shores.

"The Hippie"—the pen name for Sage Steadman, the young woman who wrote *Snowflake Obsidian: Memoir of a Cutter*— reflected on the people in her life who had acted as angels. Of them, she wrote, "They are people who have tasted sorrow, who have felt pain, and in a way, that makes them capable of being an angel. In their darkest moments they have become strong."

I think Sage is right on. As one example, I'd like to share the story of two people you've almost certainly never heard of—Natalie

Trice and her son, Lucas.[6] Lucas, now seven, was born with develop-
mental dysplasia of the hip (DDH), a malady that requires treatment
for one or two of every thousand babies affected by it. Lucas was one
of those. With very little information available about the condition
that could be readily understood by anyone but doctors, Natalie was
confused and unsure where to turn.

"When Lucas was diagnosed with DDH, I was terrified and my
initial search for information threw up horrific images and worst-case
scenarios that simply compounded my fear," Natalie recalled. Instead
of giving in to a sense of fear and helplessness, she gathered up her
strength—her perseverance, hope, perspective, courage, and, of course,
love—and decided to write a book about DDH. She did it, she said,
so other parents could "regain a little bit of control and power in what
can be a tough situation."

"It's really difficult to see your child in pain," Natalie said. "I
just wanted something positive to come out of this and provide
other parents with some kind of solace." Her book, *Cast Life: A
Parents' Guide to DDH*, was published in 2015. Just one of the
pieces of feedback she received stated, "As a parent of a child with
DDH, I had a very hard time finding useful information to help
us during this journey. Natalie Trice has written a very informative
book that is a Godsend to parents. She got a ton of feedback from
other parents on the ins and outs of hip dysplasia. I just wish this

6 The story of the Trice family was told in Dan Collinson, "Strength in Adversity," *Huff-ington Post*, February 1, 2016.

book had been around before we went through the surgeries and cast because I think it would have really helped our family."

Saying the book wouldn't have been written without Natalie's strength in the face of adversity, one reporter wrote, "Her strength of bravery enabled Natalie to be strong, so as to support her family through uncertain times and to be able to bounce back from setbacks."

The struggle isn't over for Natalie and Lucas, of course. This adversity will continue for the rest of Lucas's life, but his mother's strength will undoubtedly pull him through whatever life hands him.

Lucas isn't alone in his adversity—almost half of all American children are estimated to experience adverse situations during their childhood.[7] Not all of those involve disability or disease, of course; they also include things like their parents' divorce; living with someone who has a drug or alcohol problem; poverty; the incarceration of a parent; or physical, emotional, and sexual abuse. And while these adversities can and sometimes do lead to problems like obesity, alcoholism, drug addiction, or depression later in life, they don't always have to limit a child's eventual success. Many are able to find the strength to overcome adverse conditions and achieve stability and success. Sometimes it's as though the ones who have nothing to struggle *against* have nothing to struggle *for*.

Let's look at just a few of those who showed uncommon strength.

---

7 Vanessa Sacks, David Murphey, and Kristin Moore, "Adverse Childhood Experiences: National- and State-Level Prevalence," *Child Trends Research Brief*, July 2014, Publication #2014–28.

Ashley Judd, well-known actress and several-times Golden Globe nominee, had a troubled childhood marred by frequent adversity. As just one example, she was abused by many men, including a family member. In her memoir *All That Is Bitter and Sweet*, Judd talks about often being left on her own while her mother and sister toured the country in an effort to support the family.

Judd spoke with candid and sometimes raw detail in her memoir about her molestation and forced sexual exposure; at one time she was lured by an older man offering her a quarter to play pinball. That violent sexual assault was one of many she eventually endured.

It can't have been easy to get past the kinds of experiences Judd had. After struggling with severe depression and thoughts of suicide, she rallied her courage and leaned on the strength of her mother to determine that she would turn what happened to her into something positive—not only in terms of her own well-being but in a way she could bless the lives of others.

And that's exactly what has happened. She turned things around in a monumental way. Once the highest-paid actress in Hollywood, she is a generous philanthropist who personally participates in a number of international causes that fight against childhood sexual abuse, and she champions causes for children in the political arena. As an ambassador for YouthAIDS, she donated her time and resources to the production of three award-winning documentaries for the organization. She has also become a vocal advocate against childhood poverty and has contributed generously to many charities and foundations. She has extended her influence to issues that impact women, serving on the Leadership Council of the International Center for Research on Women.

Judd is not the only Hollywood icon who summoned uncommon strength and valor to overcome adversity in their childhood. Mark Wahlberg was once a physically violent drug addict. Shia LaBeouf grew up in such poverty he and his family traveled selling hot dogs to make ends meet; he attended Alcoholics Anonymous meetings with his father while performing stand-up routines in comedy clubs at the age of ten in an effort to help out.

Eminem, who would become the best-selling rap artist and songwriter of the decade, grew up in poverty in a trailer home, was mercilessly bullied, and endured unending domestic violence. In an interview with Oprah Winfrey, prolific actor, comedian, filmmaker, writer, and songwriter Tyler Perry said he was so relentlessly abused both physically and sexually that he "never felt safe." Reflecting on his childhood, he said, "I could go to this park in my mind that my mother and my aunt had taken me to. . . . So every time somebody was doing something to me that was horrible, that was awful, I could go to this park in my mind until it was over."

Examples of strength in adversity abound throughout history. One of the most remarkable is Frederick Douglass, who escaped slavery. Few things represent as great a trial as sheer oppression. Douglass went on to become a leading figurehead in the U.S. antislavery movement, dazzling people with his stunning oratory and impressive writing and demonstrating the stellar intellectual capacities of many of those who had been enslaved.

Betty Smith, author of *A Tree Grows in Brooklyn*, summed it up when she wrote, "Everything struggles to live. Look at that tree growing up there out of that grating. It gets no sun, and water only when it rains. It's growing out of sour earth. And it's strong because its hard struggle to live is making it strong."

Exercising Faith in Adversity

Another trait that can pull us through even the most wrenching adversity is *faith*—a concept often used in connection with religious belief (a strong conviction in God or a set of doctrines), but it's also a concept that implies complete trust or confidence in someone or something. Being able to trust in something—whether in yourself or something else—is one of the most effective ways to face adversity and transform it for good.

You've almost certainly heard the saying "It's darkest just before the dawn," but you may not have paid much attention to it (unless you have made a traumatic journey through the trials and tribulations of your own dark experience). It means exactly what it sounds like: there is hope even in the worst of circumstances.

That's what happens in nature. The darkest hour of any twenty-four-hour period is the hour just before the sun begins to inch its way toward the horizon. And what is true in nature is true of our most adverse circumstances: the darkest hour of all is the time when you think you can't go any further—the time when you are most tempted to give up. To give in to despair. It is then that the "sun"—the power of an all-loving and all-knowing God—will begin to inch its way toward your horizon, breathing new life into your battered soul, offering a new vision to your weary eyes, pointing to a new direction you had never before considered.

When you exercise the faith to accept His help, you have what you need to come out swinging. If you give up, you are guaranteed to fail. If you hang in there, if you stay in the fight, if you keep looking for the source of faith, you always have a chance to overcome even the hardest struggle. Never forget: when things seem to be at their very worst, they are about to start improving.

We've turned to the scriptures for examples before, and I'd like to do that again because that's where we find some of the most stirring examples of faith. To me, one of the most profound is that of David. As a mere youth, David was sent onto the battlefield to face Goliath—a giant of a man who was a champion in the Philistine army.

Exactly what do we mean by *giant*? No one knows with certainty because biblical scholars can't seem to agree on the meaning of the measurement given in 1 Samuel. Some say he was about six feet six inches—not anything *we* would consider gigantic but a good foot taller than the average man of the day—while others say he towered at nine feet six inches. That's closer to what most would consider a *giant*—and most of the accepted Bible translations have him in the nine-foot range.

Regardless of his exact height, we know he was considerably taller than David, who still hadn't reached his adult stature. And height was scarcely all David had to face: as described in the Bible, Goliath's bronze helmet and armor alone weighed 125 pounds (see

1 Samuel 17:5); it's mind-bending to imagine how strong someone had to be to wear that much armor. We also know Goliath carried a massive spear "like a weaver's beam," the head of the spear weighing more than fifteen pounds (v. 7). His spear and armor were so imposing that someone had to walk in front of him carrying a shield.

Saul tried to dissuade David from the confrontation: "Thou art not able to go against this Philistine to fight with him: for thou art but a youth, and he a man of war from his youth" (v. 33). Saul saw the situation for what it was—a completely unfair matchup between unequal opponents.

But David didn't see it that way. He said, "The Lord, who delivered me from the paw of the lion and from the paw of the bear, He will deliver me from the hand of this Philistine" (v. 37).

So out came David to face this behemoth on the field. He looked puny next to the Philistine warrior. He wore no armor as he had taken off that with which Saul had initially clothed him. He had, in fact, only three weapons in his arsenal: a simple sling, a few rocks, and his faith in God.

As soon as Goliath saw his opponent, he laughed. Then he taunted and cursed the youth. But David didn't back down. As the Philistine giant surveyed what he considered his almost-absurd opponent, David told him the Lord "saveth not with sword and spear: for the battle is the Lord's, and he will give you into our hands" (v. 47).

As David demonstrated next—never, ever underestimate the power of faith. David, with unwavering faith in the Lord and undoubtedly some faith in himself, reached into his bag, took out a stone, placed it in his sling, and flung it at the giant. As described in scripture, he "smote the Philistine in his forehead, that the stone sunk into his forehead; and he fell upon his face to the earth" (v. 49).

You and I are no different from David. At some time or another in your life, you will have to face your Goliath. Maybe you are standing before that Goliath right now, staring in awe at his massive size and his ominous spear and impressive suit of armor. Maybe you are face-to-face with a challenge or trial you fear may overwhelm you at any moment. In that very instant, remember two things: It is darkest just before dawn. And just as God protected and delivered David, so will He protect and deliver you.

One other account in the scriptures provides a powerful example of what faith can do in the most extreme situations. Hananiah, Mishael, and Azariah—better known as Shadrach, Meshach, and Abed-Nego—had been ordered to bow down and worship King Nebuchadnezzar's golden image.

But the three Jewish boys refused; doing so flew in the face of the first and second commandments they had been given when Moses descended from the mount carrying the stone tablets (see Exodus 20:1–6). But refusing to do so brought with it a severe consequence: if they did not worship the image, they would be thrown into a fiery furnace. And this was not a *figurative* furnace. It was the real thing, scorching flames and all.

The king—who didn't, after all, really *want* to throw them in a furnace—gave the three several chances to change their minds. After the king gave them one last chance, consider what they said to him: "O Nebuchadnezzar, we have no need to answer you in this matter. . . . Our God whom we serve is able to deliver us from the burning fiery furnace, and He will deliver us from your hand, O king. *But if not*, let it be known to you, O king, that we do not serve your gods, nor will we worship the gold image which you have set up" (Daniel 3:16–18; emphasis added).

But if not. In those three simple words is the most remarkable part of all: they knew God *could* save them from instant death in the fiery furnace. But they didn't know if He *would*. That didn't matter. Their faith was the same—strong enough to overcome any adversity and powerful enough to topple a king.

Out came the ropes. The three were bound and prepared to be burned to death. And that is exactly what happened: they were thrown into the impossibly hot, deadly furnace.

Remember how the darkest hour is just before dawn? God didn't stop the guards from tying up Shadrach, Meshach, and Abed-Nego. God didn't stop the guards from throwing the three into the furnace. God *did* stop the flames from hurting them (see Daniel 3:25–27). They walked out of the furnace unharmed, saved by their faith in an almighty God.

They hadn't known He *would*, but they trusted He *could*. You can have that same faith, and you can walk unharmed out of the furnace of your adversity in the same way.

Having Patience in Adversity

The Heidelberg Catechism instructs that we be "patient in adversity, thankful in prosperity." It's relatively easy to be thankful in prosperity, when things are going well and you have few, if any, reasons to complain. Being patient in adversity is a lot more difficult.

Patience is the ability to accept or tolerate suffering, problems, trouble, or delay without—and here's the real key—complaining or getting angry. Faced with adversity, especially unremitting adversity that seems to pull at your very soul, it's human tendency to complain. To get angry. To wonder when things will *ever* get back to normal (whatever *that* is).

If you know anything by now, you know that every one of us will eventually suffer adversity; Jesus Christ told us in no uncertain terms, "In the world ye shall have tribulation" (John 16:33). Our great challenge in life, then, is not to figure out how to *escape* affliction but how to carefully prepare to meet it and respond in ways that will bless us and the people around us.

When I suggest that patience is an important skill for dealing with adversity, I am not talking about a *passive* patience. Passive patience means you simply bide your time or wait for the passage of time to take care of the things causing you distress. Passive patience means you focus on the things happening to you. You are thrown into the position of a victim, and there you stay. It's almost as if you make a vow that you won't complain but you won't do anything to really help yourself, either.

I am suggesting an *active* patience, one in which you assess your situation and decide on a plan and make things happen. You persist with determination. You stand firm in your resolve that you will gather up your resources and gain an understanding of what's causing your adversity and how you can best resolve it. You react, as Paul described to the Romans, "by patient continuance in well doing" (Romans 2:7).

Rarely is the road a smooth and even one. Many who have enjoyed tremendous success have had to exercise great patience along the way. One of those is George Herman "Babe" Ruth, who grew up in an apartment above his father's saloon. At the tender age of seven, he was sent to St. Mary's Industrial School for Boys—an orphanage and reform school—where he stayed for the next twelve years. At the school, he was expected to learn a skill. He became a carpenter and shirtmaker. And he learned to play baseball.

It took unmeasured patience to rise above those beginnings, but Babe Ruth found a way. He started out as a star pitcher. But as he developed his skills and stuck with it, he achieved his real fame as the "Sultan of Swat," hitting 714 home runs and driving in 2,213 runs in the twenty-two seasons of his baseball career. The result of his patience? He became one of the greatest baseball players of all time. A sign of his ongoing patience? He often maintained that he never let a strikeout discourage him from his next chance at bat.

Born into slavery in 1856, Booker T. Washington was well acquainted with hardship. He also knew a lot about emerging triumphant from adversity: when he was freed by the Emancipation

Proclamation, he moved to West Virginia and patiently worked in the coal mines while he earned enough money to get an education.

After years of patient determination, he went east to Hampton Institute, a school established to educate freed slave men. He worked harder than he had ever worked. The result of his patience? He went on to become the first leader of the Tuskegee Institute in Alabama, where he served for the rest of his life as one of the foremost national leaders for African-Americans and a prominent voice for former slaves and their descendants. One of the sentiments for which he is best known refers to his patience in overcoming adversity: "Success isn't measured by the position you reach in life; it's measured by the obstacles you overcome."

French fashion designer and businesswoman Gabrielle Bonheur Chanel—you know her as Coco Chanel—is one of the world's most influential designers. With a line of couture clothing, jewelry, handbags, and fragrances (including the iconic Chanel No. 5), she is the only fashion designer on *Time* magazine's list of the one hundred most influential people of the twentieth century.

But things weren't always that way—and they didn't come easily for Coco. She was born in 1883 to an unmarried mother who worked in a charity hospital as a laundress. Her father was an itinerant street vendor who peddled work clothing. It didn't take a genius to see that as things stood, Coco's future didn't look particularly promising.

But anyone who clung to that notion didn't know Coco and didn't understand her grit, determination, vision, and patience. At the age of six—when most children couldn't even reach the pedals on a sewing machine—she learned to sew. She meticulously honed her skill until she was able to get a job as a seamstress.

From there, fate seemed to smile upon the young girl. As she patiently established relationships in the industry, she got the opportunity to begin designing hats. From there, she worked into a position where she was able to design deluxe casual clothing. Her patience finally paid off when she was able to open her own fashion boutique in Paris, which ultimately led to her fame and influence.

Had she wallowed in her early desperate circumstances, she may not have seen much to which she could aspire. But she wasn't one to give up, and she had the patience to stay the course. Coco's own story, forged by patience and hard work, inspired her to say, "Success is often achieved by those who don't know that failure is inevitable."

The greatest example of patience in dealing with adversity, of course, is Jesus Christ. He was rejected, spit upon, reviled, cast to the wolves; indeed, as it was said of Him, "The foxes have holes, and the birds of the air have nests; but the Son of man hath not where to lay his head" (Matthew 8:20). Ultimately, he was nailed to a cross and crucified after suffering for the sins of all the world. Clearly, He suffered more than any of us will ever suffer at an extreme we will never know.

We know all too well our initial reaction when we are pummeled by the worst life has to offer. In contrast, look at the way He patiently dealt with what He was given: "When he was reviled, he did not revile in return; when he suffered, he did not threaten, but continued entrusting himself to him who judges justly" (1 Peter 2:23). In other words, He knew His Father had not left Him alone. He trusted God with His suffering. And if you exercise patience, you can do the same—because God will never leave *you* alone either.

One of the greatest examples of patience in adversity is Christ's own prayer in the Garden of Gethsemane. There, knowing full well what lay ahead of Him, He cried out in fervent prayer: "O my Father, if it be possible, let this cup pass from me: nevertheless not as I will, but as thou wilt" (Matthew 26:39).

Look at that sublime example. In the midst of extreme distress and unremitting adversity, we may plead, "Let this cup pass from me." In those moments, our "cup" may consist of unemployment, abuse, divorce, financial ruin, sickness, pain, anxiety, betrayal, depression, the loss or death of a loved one, or so many of the other adversities that beset us.

But how often do we continue, as Jesus did, with the sincere statement: "Nevertheless not as I will, but as thou wilt?" The key word in that supplication is *nevertheless*. It means you have enough faith to place your all in the hands of the Lord—and the patience to see what that will eventually look like.

As you struggle with adversity—because you will; we all do—never forget God. He is an important part of the sublime arithmetic that allows you to face and transform adversity, to come out of it a better, stronger, more qualified soul. Focus on God, not your adversity. Find God in every part of your adversity because He will be there. In fact, chances are good He will use your adversity to display His glory as you depend on Him and exercise faith in Him.

And never forget that adversity may actually be a gift from God.

You read that right. I had to reach the tender young age of sixty before I realized that every trial, every tribulation, and every other situation in life (including the good ones!) were literally gifts from God. I had always heard He had a sense of humor, but I didn't really understand what that meant. I sure do now.

Now that you know a little more about adversity and how to handle it, you'll recognize something you've probably always known: that God gives us much good. But I hope you also know that God also gives us the bad and the ugly because they are wake-up calls that bring us closer to Him. And as we draw closer to Him, we realize He can stop the bleeding and very literally protect us from some unseen disaster approaching over the next hill.

Your job is to accept *all* the gifts God has for you: the good, the bad, and the ugly. The good? That's a no-brainer. The bad? The bad things are still gifts because they cause you to come up with different ways of doing things; they blast you out of your comfort zone, and you usually end up growing as a result. And the ugly? The ugly things make you think outside the box as you look for the good—and if they're ugly enough, they drive you to God in your quest for help and comfort. Welcome all of them, even the gifts you never would have chosen for yourself. God, in His infinite wisdom, knows *exactly* which gifts will give you the greatest growth and blessings, and that's what He sends.

Whatever you do, stop worrying about what the future holds: "For God hath not given us the spirit of fear; but of power, and of love, and of a sound mind" (1 Timothy 1:7). I don't care how smart you are: there's no way of predicting what will happen next year, next month, or even tomorrow. But God can and does. All kinds of things will happen that will catch you off guard because God will follow the exact plan He has laid out for you. As I said earlier, you may not know what that plan is, but He does. Trust Him to execute it with perfect judgment for your greatest growth—even when it seems uglier than anything you could have imagined. Remember that as well when it seems more beautiful and sublime than anything you could have imagined, because God will send you both. Your success and what you make of your life will depend on how you respond to the things He sends. Again I say, "Change your perception, change your life."

And above all, remember that you are not alone.

That's often easier said than done. When you feel the weight of the world pressing down on your shoulders, when you are facing insurmountable odds, when you are staring tribulation in the face, it's easy to feel alone. When you spend every shred of time and effort and energy taking care of everyone else—your children, your husband, your aging parents—without a word of thanks, it's easy to feel alone. When you work all day at an office and never seem to get anything done, only to go home to a sink full of dirty dishes and a pile of dirty laundry and impish grins on dirty faces, it's easy to feel alone. When you lose a job, lose a spouse, lose a child, lose a piece of your heart, it's easy to feel alone.

At those times, remember the example I gave earlier of what the Apostle Paul wrote to the Corinthians: "We are hard pressed on every side, but not crushed; perplexed, but not in despair; persecuted, but not abandoned; struck down, but not destroyed" (2 Corinthians 4:8–9). And as you feel those same things—hard pressed, perplexed, persecuted, even struck down—remember that no one ever sinks too low for the rescuing power of God. "And the God of all grace . . . after you have suffered a little while, will himself restore you and make you strong, firm and steadfast" (2 Peter 5:10). That is a promise from a God who never breaks His promises.

No, you are not alone. You will never be alone. Every smile in the grocery store checkout line, every hand on your shoulder, every shared tear comes from someone who has also suffered adversity. I know this because *we all have.* Today may be your turn to receive comfort from one who has walked a mile in your moccasins, far down the path ahead of you. Tomorrow it may be your turn to come back from your treacherous journey, stronger and better and more sure, to provide that comfort to someone else.

This adversity—this one, the next one, and the one after that— will never be the end. It is the beginning. If you let it, it will make of you a magnificent creature, more than you ever could have accomplished on your own.

C.S. Lewis said it much more eloquently than I can:

Imagine yourself as a living house. God comes in to rebuild that house. At first, perhaps, you can understand what He is doing. He is getting the drains right and stopping the leaks in the roof and so on; you knew that those jobs needed doing and so you are not surprised. But presently He starts knocking the house about in a way that hurts abominably and does not seem to make any sense. What on earth is He up to? The explanation is that He is building quite a different house from the one you thought of—throwing out a new wing here, putting on an extra floor there, running up towers, making courtyards. You thought you were being made into a decent little cottage: but He is building a palace. He intends to come and live in it Himself.

Chapter Three

Failure Propels You to Success: Quitting Is Not an Option

When you get into a tight place and everything goes
against you, till it seems as though you could not hang
on a minute longer, never give up then, for that is just
the place and time that the tidewill turn.

—*Harriet Beecher Stowe*

I'm pretty well acquainted with failure. I think we all are. I've made some mistakes, some of them pretty stupid ones. I think lots of people can relate to that, too. Look at something as simple as New Year's resolutions: a study by *Inc.* magazine says that a staggering 92 percent of people who set goals at the beginning of the year never achieve them.[8] In fact, eight out of ten bail on those goals within a month.[9]

---

8 Marcel Schwantes, "Science Says 92 Percent of People Don't Achieve Their Goals. Here's How the Other 8 Percent Do," *Inc.*
9 Kelsey Mulvey, "80% of New Year's Resolutions Fail by February," *Business Insider*, January 3, 2017.

Businesses don't do much better. Nine out of ten startups fail. In fact, wrote one entrepreneur and expert, the situation is so grim "entrepreneurs may even want to write their failure post-mortem before they launch their business."[10] Fast-forward five years down the road, and only half of all small businesses still have their doors open.[11]

I know all about failure. I've been up close and personal with it plenty of times. You may have been too. You may even be staring at it right now. But I *also* know failure is *not* the end. And I know quitting is *not* an option. I know this because my own experience shouts it. And if my experience isn't enough to persuade you that failure is *not* the end and that you should never quit, I've got some pretty convincing examples of people who stared failure right in the face and used that experience to become some of the world's most dynamic successes.

These are people you've heard of. Household names.

And while you've heard of *them* and their breathtaking successes, you may *not* have heard of their failures. So let's take a look at a few.

When it comes to failure, Abraham Lincoln may just be the poster child. Every American knows Abraham Lincoln was president of the United States. He was elected in 1860, the sixteenth man to hold the highest office in the country. His election came at a perilous time in the nation's history: we were teetering on the

---

10 Neil Patel, "90% of Startups Fail: Here's What You Need to Know about the 10%," *Forbes*, January 16, 2015.
11 Georgia McIntyre, "What Percentage of Small Businesses Fail?: And Other Similar Stats You Need to Know, *Fundera*, August 29, 2017.

brink of civil war, and he couldn't help but realize he had a monumental task ahead of him.

Not quite two years after taking office, he issued the Emancipation Proclamation, reshaping the cause of the Civil War. Once an effort to save the Union, the war was transformed by Lincoln's inspired vision into an instrument aimed at abolishing slavery.

For just a minute, let's focus not on the years of his tremendously successful presidency but on the three decades that preceded it. His failures during those years had to have been disheartening at best. In 1831, he failed in business; the next year, he ran for the state legislature and was defeated. In 1833, he started a new business—and it too failed. In 1835, his fiancée died; on the heels of that loss, he suffered a nervous breakdown.

Pulling himself up by his bootstraps, he ran for Congress in 1843. He was defeated. In 1848, he made another congressional bid; again he was defeated. In 1855, he ran for the Senate. He lost. The next year he was on the ticket as candidate for vice president of the United States. Once again he lost. In 1859, he made yet another bid for the Senate. Yet again he was defeated.

That's a dismally *long* string of defeats. My experiences pale in comparison, and yours probably do too. But if you can take anything from Abraham Lincoln, take this: what matters most is not how many times you fail but that you never stop trying. Because a year after that sixth election loss—*sixth!*—he was elected president of the United States.

Considering his track record before that landmark election, Abraham Lincoln had ample cause to consider himself a failure. But there's no way *anyone* can consider his presidency a failure. Besides leading the Union to victory in the Civil War and issuing the Emancipation Proclamation, his four short years in the White House were characterized by his establishment of the national banking system, the U. S. Department of Agriculture, and various measures that led to the Reconstruction. He signed the Homestead Act, giving small tracts of land to farmers, and the Land Grant College Act, giving states public lands on which they could build universities that specialized in agriculture, mechanics, and military tactics.

And the next time you dive in to your turkey dinner, remember that Abraham Lincoln signed the Thanksgiving Proclamation, establishing Thanksgiving as a national holiday.

No. This man was no failure. In fact, take a look at how he did in a rating of America's presidents.[12] More than seven hundred elected officials, professors, historians, attorneys, authors, and other respected figures participated in a poll rating the nation's presidents on things like leadership qualities, accomplishments, political skill, crisis management, character, and integrity. Abraham Lincoln finished first. (Franklin D. Roosevelt came in second, and George Washington rounded out the top three.)

A separate poll sponsored by C-SPAN and released in February 2009 asked sixty-five historians to rank America's presidents in

---

12   William J. Ridings, Jr. and Stuart B. McIver, *Rating the Presidents* (Secaucus, NJ: Citadel Press, 1997).

ten categories ranging from economic management and public persuasion to moral authority and international relations. Again, Abraham Lincoln finished first. (This time George Washington came in second, and Franklin D. Roosevelt finished third.)

I don't think even the most hardened critic could consider that a failure.

Abraham Lincoln accomplished what he did because he refused to let failure keep him down. No matter how many times he faced defeat, he got back up. Got back into the fray. Drove himself to try again. And in trying again, he shaped the destiny of a nation.

Here's the remarkable thing: He's not the only one who faced failure after failure before he reached into the depths of his soul and realized astonishing success. Scattered throughout this chapter, you'll look at a few dozen others who demonstrate how failure can be a powerful prelude to success.

Here's what these people know that you and I need to remember: If you're afraid to fail, you can't possibly succeed. You'll find yourself paralyzed. Terrified. Scared to do anything at all because it might not work. *You* might not work. And so there you stay, stuck forever.

And what about this: What if you've *already* failed? What if you put your all into it, and despite your best efforts you fell flat on your face? What, then?

Remember Abraham Lincoln? You get back up. You dust yourself off. You praise God for what you learned as a result. And with His help, you keep on trying.

Let's look at another household name whose initial experiences were riddled with failure. Oprah Winfrey's (my girl, my mentor) start in life couldn't have been less promising: she was born in 1950s rural Mississippi to an impoverished teenage mother—not exactly the best situation. Believe it or not, things went downhill from there. She endured chronic abuse at the age of nine. At thirteen, she ran away from home. At fourteen, she became pregnant; the baby died shortly after birth. With just that alone, imagine the naysayers. Never allow the naysayers and their negativity to steal your dreams. To naysayers, I say, "I'm on a mission, so get thee behind me."

No one could argue that things were looking pretty bad at that point, but Oprah didn't let that get her down. She moved in with her father in Tennessee. Determined to make something of herself, she got high marks in school, participated in speech and debate, and won a state beauty pageant. She did all that while working part-time reading the news at a local radio station. With grit and determination, she earned a scholarship to Tennessee State University, where she thrived as a communications major.

Imagine her relief. Maybe, just maybe, her failures were behind her.

Not so.

Her first job after graduation was at a station in Nashville, and that led to a job with ABC affiliate WJZ-TV in Baltimore, where she was hired in a prime-time slot as co-anchor of the evening news alongside veteran anchor Jerry Turner. That would have been an incredible coup for any broadcast journalist, but it was especially so for Oprah Winfrey—a young black woman in a world ruled by old white men. The station, wanting to attract a broader and more diverse audience for the news, went on an all-out promotional campaign for weeks, thrusting Oprah into the spotlight before she even started and creating impossibly high expectations.

Of the promotional campaign, Oprah herself said, "I was on the back of buses. I was on billboards. . . . And what happened is that when I arrived, people were expecting this big something. The buildup was so strong. And I'm just a colored girl with a lot of hair sitting next to Jerry Turner, and everybody's like, 'Whaaaaaaaaattttt? That's what an Oprah is? She's not all that.'"[13]

It was a recipe for disaster. And failure. Throughout her all-too-brief stint as coanchor, she faced sexism and harassment. But there was more. Not only did she fail to meet the public's expectations, she had a spectacular and ruinous personality clash with Jerry Turner— who, as it turns out, never wanted a co-anchor to begin with. The show failed in record time, to no one's surprise, and Oprah took the brunt of the blame. No one even cast any culpability on Turner, who was anything but accommodating to her. She was dropped after just a few months and subsequently shuffled through a string of lower-level jobs—reading headlines on the air (similar to what she'd done in high school), reporting here and there, and writing copy.

Though she was determined and stayed focused, even *that* didn't work out for her. She wasn't a fast enough writer; producers constantly yelled at her to pick up the pace. She didn't fare much better

---

13 Jeff Stibel, "Oprah Winfrey: A Profile in Failure," *Linked In.*

as a reporter. Though she hated TV news, she loved human-interest stories—yet found herself unable to stay emotionally detached. In one memorable episode, she did a story on a family whose house had burned down. She was so touched by their plight that the next day she took them some of her own blankets and other household goods. Her director was furious. Such a thing was against the rules, he said—and if she did it again, he would fire her.

Winfrey herself called those early years at WJZ-TV the "first and worst failure" of her TV career. It's not hard to see why. But what happened next was far from what would be considered typical. "Most people in her shoes would have changed into boots, pursued a different career, quit, given up, something other than persist. But in retrospect, the lessons learned from her time in Baltimore were invaluable and she used those lessons to hone her compass and point her in the right direction, rather than change course."[14]

The two biggest lessons she took from that "failure"? First, she was invested in human-interest pieces—stories about people that went straight to the heart. And second, she loved the idea of being a host—and didn't want to have a cohost unless she felt a deep and abiding connection with that person.

Bundling up those hard-earned lessons, she was tapped for a local Baltimore TV talk show, *People Are Talking*, with Richard Sher—and the two had an instant chemistry. She stayed in that gig—which many would have considered a demoralizing demotion—for five years, demonstrating her ability to resonate with and engage

14 Stibel, "Oprah Winfrey: A Profile in Failure."

viewers. From there, she was recruited to host a morning talk show in Chicago—and the rest, as they say, is history. Within two years, the show achieved national syndication, bumping the nation's most popular talk-show host, Phil Donahue, down in the ratings.

"Every Strike Brings Me Closer"

You probably think of the legendary Babe Ruth as one of the greatest baseball players of all time. Most do—his home-run record stood unchallenged for thirty-four years and launched him into baseball's Hall of Fame. But here's something you probably didn't know: when he retired in 1935, he also held the record for the most strikeouts in all of major-league baseball. Here's what that means: He slogged back to the dugout in defeat twice as often as he ran the bases in victory. But he never focused on those failures. As he put it, "I just go up there and I swing. I just keep on swinging and I keep on swinging. Every strike brings me closer to my next home run."

With the *Oprah Winfrey Show*, which led the ratings for twenty-five years, she became the undisputed queen of television talk shows—then amassed a media empire, including her own television network. Catapulted from obscurity to one of the wealthiest and most influential people in America, she is now worth an estimated $2.9 billion, according to *Forbes* magazine.

Not bad for a poor girl born in the least advantageous circumstances imaginable and who endured one failure after another. And it's all due to the fact that she refused to let failure define her—refused to be defeated when she knew she could get back up and keep trying.

British adventurer, writer, and Northern Ireland television star Edward Michael "Bear" Grylls, one of the most celebrated survivalists in the world, says, "Survival can be summed up in three words—never give up. That's the heart of it, really. Just keep trying." His mantra is simple: Be brave. Inquisitive. Prepared for the journey. Ready for anything. *Unafraid to fail.*

Never be afraid of failure. It is your best tool for success.

If that seems counterintuitive, consider this: once you fail, you've failed. It's all uphill from there. You don't have to worry about failing anymore because you've done it. It's over. You're free to go anywhere you want and to do anything you set your mind to, all without fear. Fear cripples. Failure endows you with the freedom to succeed—to create a new life as you walk (or run) away from the *I can't* attitude you carried before that failure.

Everyone fails. The ones who end up being successful have one simple characteristic in common: they refuse to give up.

Oprah Winfrey is far from the only entertainer ever stymied by failure but who refused to quit trying. Check out a few others. The four British chaps who named themselves the Beatles enjoyed limited success playing cover songs in bars and clubs but were turned down by almost every record label they approached. The most famous—and foolhardy—of those rejections came from Decca Records, where an executive refused to sign the group because "guitar groups are on the way out" and "the Beatles have no future in show business."

Decca's dumping of the Beatles is still considered one of the biggest mistakes in music history. *No success in show business?* According to *Rolling Stone* magazine, the Beatles showed up that Decca exec by capturing the first five slots on the Billboard Singles chart in the same week. Their music hit number-one status in thirty-five countries. They had the best-selling album of the twenty-first century to date. And they went on to sell more than a billion records.

Just guessing here, but I'd call that "success in show business." And it seems Decca learned its lesson. Just two years after the label rejected the Beatles, guitarist George Harrison offered Decca execs a tip: sign the Rolling Stones. And so another legend was born.

Then there's actor Harrison Ford. He arrived in Hollywood filled with hope and determination and landed a bit part—that of a bellboy—in the 1996 film *Dead Heat on a Merry-Go-Round*. He was paid only $150 a week. After filming was over, the director took Ford into his office and told him, "You'll never make it in this business." Ford didn't have any of the ingredients for success, he was told. He might as well give it up.

He refused. To give up, that is. He took a job as a carpenter to help make ends meet and kept at it, auditioning for one film after another and working to hone his skills. His career went on to span six decades, including timeless roles in blockbusters like the *Indiana Jones* and *Star Wars* series, the last installment of which broke an array of box-office records.

Considered one of Hollywood's most bankable stars, by the mid-1990s Ford was earning $20 million per film and collecting 15 percent of the film's gross take at the box office. Good thing he didn't listen to the shortsighted director who predicted he'd never make it in show business.

The same thing has happened throughout the decades to all kinds of entertainers. Lucille Ball was in so many poorly rated films at the start of her career she became known as the "Queen of B Movies"— not a title to which anyone aspires. But she wasn't discouraged by that string of failures. She kept trying and got her big break when CBS turned her and her husband, Desi Arnaz's, vaudeville act into the wildly successful sitcom *I Love Lucy*. An estimated 44 million viewers—72 percent of all those with televisions in their homes—tuned in to the episode in which Lucy gave birth to Little Ricky.

The series endured for 179 episodes and created one of the most prolific and influential television production companies of the 1950s. When it ceased production as a weekly series in 1957, *I Love Lucy* was still the number-one series in the nation. It still captures top ratings in reruns.

Then there's celebrated dancer Fred Astaire. An aspiring actor, he was thrilled to finally get a screen test with MGM Studios. That thrill could have been demolished when he received the director's feedback on his audition, which, according to the *Chicago Tribune*, read: "Can't act. Can't sing. Slightly bald. Not handsome. Can dance a little."

Astaire refused to take that judgment sitting down. In fact, he spent the rest of his career proving that executive wrong as he sang, danced, and acted his way through some of America's most beloved musicals, appearing in an astonishing 212 dance numbers. He later created a chain of successful dance studios.

Can dance a little? Perhaps one of the biggest understatements ever made. After he became a colossal success, Astaire displayed the director's note in his Beverly Hills mansion, where he looked at it often to remind himself to never take *no* for an answer.

Bouncing Back from Rejection

Just twenty years ago, Shawn Corey Carter was an unsigned rapper who sold his mixtapes out of the trunk of his car. Today, the rapper known as Jay-Z has released twelve platinum albums, won fourteen Grammy Awards, and has amassed a fortune estimated to be in the high nine figures.

Not bad for a kid from New York's infamous Marcy Projects. Also not bad for a guy who was turned down by every record label in the business. They said he was too old. Too "soft" (he didn't rap about drugs or crime). Just didn't have what it took.

Instead of focusing on rejection and giving up, he was determined to dream "enormous" and refused to take his eye off the prize. Failing at his first plan, he went to plan B, forming his own record label to release his first album.

Describing himself as a "hustler"—an energetic go-getter—he advises others, "Without the work, the magic won't come."

And don't forget Sidney Poitier. Born prematurely in Florida and raised in the Bahamas, he grew up in unremitting poverty on a tiny island with no electricity, running water, paved roads, automobiles, or other modern conveniences. He left school at the age of twelve to help support his family, who was selling tomatoes. At the age of fifteen, he moved to the United States to live with his brother after his best friend was sent to reform school.

In his first audition for the American Negro Theatre, Poitier spoke in a heavy Caribbean accent and messed up his lines so badly the director angrily told Poitier to stop wasting his time. In fact, the director's exact words were "Why don't you stop wasting people's time and go out and become a dishwasher or something?" That would seem like a failure in anyone's book—but Poitier had a dream, and he refused to let failure stand in his way. He offered to work as an unpaid janitor at the theatre in exchange for acting classes.

Refusing to let his failed audition determine his future, he doggedly worked on his craft and eventually became one of the most highly respected and successful people in the business. He was the first African-American to win a Best Actor Academy Award, receive an award at a top international film festival (the Venice Film Festival), and be a top-grossing movie star in the United States. In 2001, he received a special Oscar for Lifetime Achievement in motion pictures. And in 2009, he was awarded the Presidential Medal of Freedom, the nation's highest civilian honor.

No longer could he be accused of wasting *anyone's* time.

Academy Award-winning director Steven Spielberg—described by teachers as "an intelligent but awkward and geeky kid" who was bullied by his classmates—was rejected by the University of Southern California School of Cinematic Arts multiple times. But he looked at those failures as mere obstacles on his road to success—going on to create the first summer blockbuster, *Jaws*, in 1975, and becoming the most successful movie director of all time with *Close Encounters of the Third Kind, Indiana Jones, E.T., Poltergeist, The Color Purple, Schindler's List*, and *Saving Private Ryan*.

As one writer described him, "When Steven didn't get into the prestigious film schools, he didn't take the rejection personally. He simply charted a different path to his goal. When he was kicked off a movie set, he didn't call the plan a failure. He just moved over to another set. When he was told to shoot his film in another format, he didn't let the obstacle stop him. He accepted the challenge and shot the film again . . . and again."[15]

What these gifted entertainers—and so many others—realized is that failure crops up in a variety of situations. But that's the key: failure is a *situation*. You can't change a situation. That's so important I'm going to say it again: *You can't change a situation*. The only thing you can change is *yourself*.

Steven Spielberg couldn't change the fact that a prestigious film school refused to admit him. Sidney Poitier couldn't change the opinion of a director who maintained his efforts were a waste

---

15 Doug Stevenson, "Get Out of Your Own Way," reprinted in Stacey Mayo, "How Steven Spielberg Became Remarkably Successful," *balancedliving.com*.

of time. Lucille Ball couldn't change the fact that she was cast only in B-rated movies. Jay-Z couldn't change the fact that record labels refused to produce his music. Fred Astaire couldn't change the fact that his audition was panned by a director who deemed him unsuitable for just about everything.

But those people could—and *did*—change themselves. Most important, they took *responsibility* for changing themselves. Sidney Poitier took acting classes and paid for them in exchange for janitorial work. Jay-Z, determined to produce his album, started his own label to do it. Harrison Ford kept going out on auditions and working on his skills.

Each of these people changed themselves, and their situations changed as a result. None of them let failure be the defining factor. None of them listened to rejection. All of them, as Jay-Z put it, dreamed "enormous." And all of them achieved enormous.

Failure Makes You Smarter

Failure can do a lot of things for you—and we've already looked at some of them. It can make you more determined. Give you the guts to move forward. Cement in your heart and soul the refusal to give up.

But did you know it can actually make you smarter?

That's not just me talking. It's based on scientific research, and the results are compelling.

Before we look at that science, let's take a look at a few scientists who overcame their own bouts with failure. These five standouts will continue making a case for failure and what it can do for you.

Let's start with Sir Isaac Newton. In a misguided plan if there ever was one, his mother pulled him out of school when he was just a boy so he could run the family farm. He failed miserably. *Miserably.*

Some would have taken that failure as a general commentary on his abilities for everything else, too. But Isaac begged to go back to school because he knew he could do other things. Then he persuaded his mother to let him enroll in Cambridge University.

Newton went on to become one of the greatest scientists of all time, revolutionizing physics and mathematics. In addition to his work on gravity, he developed the three laws of motion that are the basis of modern physics, and he discovered calculus. So much for his failures on the family farm.

Thomas Edison is almost legendary for his inventions—but should be almost as well-regarded for his failures. When all was said and done, he held more than a thousand patents and invented a number of devices that literally changed the world, including the incandescent light bulb, the phonograph, a movie camera, the Dictaphone, the world's first electric lamp, and the kinetoscope. He also greatly improved the telephone by inventing the carbon microphone.

Sounds like an amazingly accomplished man, and he was. But there were plenty of failures along the way. Consider this: Edison made a thousand unsuccessful attempts at inventing the light bulb before he came up with one that worked. Hearing of the process, a reporter chided him by asking, "How did it feel to fail 1,000 times?"

"I didn't fail 1,000 times," Edison responded. "The light bulb was an invention with 1,000 steps."

On another occasion, he said, "Great success is built on failure, frustration, even catastrophe. I have not failed. I've just found 10,000 ways that won't work."

Telling audiences that the key to success is finding a better way to do anything, Edison said something that should resound with all of us: "Our greatest weakness lies in giving up. The most certain way to succeed is always to try just one more time."

"Failure Is Success in Progress"

When he was a child, no one would have considered Albert Einstein . . . well, an Einstein. He had difficulty communicating and learning in a traditional manner. His parents thought he was "sub-normal," and one of his teachers described him as "mentally slow, unsociable, and adrift forever in foolish dreams." He was expelled from school. He finally did learn to speak and read, and even to do a little math.

But he never let any of it get him down. "Anyone who has never made a mistake has never tried anything new," he maintained. He kept trying new things, and kept making mistakes. But he built on those mistakes and eventually was awarded the Nobel Prize in physics for, among other things, his discovery of the theory of relativity.

That *one more time* can make all the difference. Another prominent inventor had a situation similar to that of Edison, though his failures may have been even more fabled. In attempting to develop his vacuum, Sir James Dyson went through *5,126* failed prototypes and used all his savings during the fifteen years he struggled.

But he kept trying, just as Edison advised. And the 5,127th prototype worked. Dyson went on to become the best-selling bagless vacuum brand in the United States. According to *Forbes*, the man who refused to give up after more than five thousand failures is now worth an estimated $4.5 billion.

And what about Charles Darwin? He wanted to be a physician, but his academic performance just didn't cut it. Abandoning his career in medicine, he decided to go to school to become a parson—a member of the clergy, more commonly known as a rector or vicar. But deciding not to give up on the sciences, Darwin put aside his academic failures and focused on his studies of nature. He subsequently traveled the world to uncover the mysteries of nature. His writings—especially his pioneering *On the Origin of the Species*—rocked the scientific community and introduced the theory of evolution.

These were all, without question, very, very smart people. And they all had more than their share of failures. Knowing what we know now, it's a good bet those failures contributed to the intelligence that enabled them to change the world.

Here's how it works.[16] Consider the way you traditionally learned in the classroom. Your teacher introduced something to

---

16 Discussion of this scientific evidence is from Jeff Stibel, "The Science Behind Failure: How It Actually Makes You Smarter," *Linked In*, December 10, 2014.

you, showed you how to do it, and then let you practice. That's a proven method of teaching everything from tying shoes to turning on a light to solving algebra equations to reciting historical dates. But the results of an experiment recently published in *Cognitive Science*[17] may cause us to reconsider that way of doing things—and give us a lot to think about when it comes to failure.

In the experiment, groups of students were taught to solve math problems. The first group was taught the traditional way: the teacher introduced the concept, taught the students how to solve the problem, and then let them practice. Things were done in a radically different way with the second group. Those students were given the problems to solve on their own; no one introduced the concept or showed them how to solve the problems until *after* they had tried several times to work things out on their own.

At first glance, the results weren't that surprising. Students in both groups ultimately learned how to solve the problems.

But that's where the similarity stopped. Upon closer examination, the results were striking. The students in the second group— the ones who had to try it out on their own first and who had to try and fail a few times before getting it right—had a "significantly greater conceptual understanding" of the math. Not only that, but they were able to transfer what they had learned to other problems much better than the students in the first group.

---

17 Manu Kapur, "Productive Failure in Learning Math," *Cognitive Science* 38, no. 5 (June 2014), 1008–22.

The students in the second group didn't come to their knowledge by the wave of a magic wand. In fact, they almost never figured out the solutions on their own; someone still had to show them. *But the act of trying and failing gave them a deeper understanding of the problems and their solutions.* In other words, when someone shows you the right way to do something before you do it, you memorize the information—but may not necessarily understand it. When you have to stumble around and fumble a little (in other words, fail) first, that knowledge gets thoroughly embedded in your mind. The next time you encounter something similar, regardless of the situation, you *get it*.

A reporter commenting on the study said, "The message is clear. Get out there and fail, but make it about learning, not risk taking. It's what our brains evolved to do, and it's the only way to get exceptionally good at anything."[18] In other words, failure *does* make you smarter. And when you're smarter, you have a greater chance to succeed.

While it's making you smarter, failure also does some other important things for you. That's if you approach it well.

Start by recognizing—really accepting—that everyone fails. It's a universal experience. No one is immune. And it's nothing to be ashamed of. A couple of years ago, two innovative employees at LinkedIn started what they called the "Failure Wall."[19] They sneaked in after hours and used permanent markers to write a

---

18 Stibel, "The Science Behind Failure."
19 Jeff Stibel, "Two Years of Failure," LinkedIn, December 11, 2013.

bunch of quotes about failure on a large wall. After one of them left, the other wrote some of his "most humbling failures" on the wall.

Other employees saw it right away. As it caught on, others— employees, partners, and even family members—came and added their failures to the wall. Soon it was absolutely littered with failures. Before long, the press caught wind of it; it was featured with mixed reviews on NPR's *Here and Now,* in the *Los Angeles Times,* and in *HuffPost Live.*

Reflecting on the wall two years later, the original contributor learned four important things about failure. The first is that failure helps you grow and innovate. Quickly. If you want to get better at what you do, want to pull yourself out of a rut, want to succeed, fail. It's the best tool you have.

The second is that we should all feel safe in admitting our failures. Remember Edison? He didn't blanch when asked how he felt going through a thousand prototypes for the light bulb. He didn't need to. He realized he wasn't the first to experience failure, nor would he be the last. He also knew those failures led to success— something you can remember every time you screw in a light bulb.

The third thing the Failure Wall demonstrated is that old failures disappear once they are acknowledged. Those who wrote on the wall used "permanent" markers, but those failures might not live up to their name very well because within a few months the failures that were jotted down started to fade. Within about nine months, they had completely vanished. And that's what happens with failure. Acknowledge it, and it's no longer front and center in your mind. It starts to fade as you focus on other things—like how you're going to build on that failure to accomplish something wonderful. Get it out. Let it go.

Finally, the Failure Wall taught that failure is really no big deal. Acknowledge it, learn from it, and try not to repeat it, and what happens from there can be the stuff of miracles. After stumbling along for a while, you will suddenly experience an *Aha!* moment, and what happens next may very literally change the course of history—if not the nation's, at least yours.

That's what happened to a number of prominent business leaders who floundered around with one failure after another before landing the success for which they are remembered. Get ready for some more household names, because you're certain to recognize these—if not for their failures, for their dramatic successes.

Colonel Harland David Sanders had what we might call a "troubled" employment history; over the years, he was fired from dozens of jobs. Then he finally landed on an idea he really thought would work: he developed a recipe for fried chicken using—and you're sure to have heard this line—"eleven herbs and spices." He thought it was finger-lickin' good and banked on others feeling the same way. They didn't.

He traversed the country trying to sell his chicken at more than a thousand different restaurants. None agreed that his recipe was anything special; not a single one agreed to carry it as a menu item. More than a few cracked jokes about his bow tie and starched white suit.

It would have been easy, even natural, for the colonel to give up. That was *more than a thousand* rejections. But he kept going. And what happened next was exactly what he had dreamed of: a business deal in Utah came through, and today there are more than eighteen thousand Kentucky Fried Chicken franchises around the world.

Sometimes you have to use failure to move you from one plan to another. Vera Wang had always dreamed of competing on the U.S. figure-skating team in the Olympics. She didn't make the team. That was a situation she couldn't change, so she moved on to plan B: she set her sights on the top position at *Vogue* and was hired as an editor at the prestigious publication. Once again, she failed—she was passed over for promotion to the position of editor-in-chief. It was another situation she couldn't change.

But she *could* change her goals, and she moved on to plan C. Leveraging what she learned from her first two failures, she came up with a strategy. At the age of forty, she entered an industry dominated by those much younger, and she began designing wedding gowns. Today she is one of the premier designers in the fashion industry, with a business worth more than $1 billion.

Wang wasn't the only one who changed direction midstream. Bill Gates and Paul Allen put their talents together and started a business called Traf-O-Data. Positioning traffic counters throughout urban areas, they translated the raw data they collected, generated it into valuable reports, and sold those reports to cities throughout the state of Washington for traffic-planning purposes. It was genius. And almost as suddenly it was pointless:

the state started giving the reports away for free. Almost as quickly as it had started, the business model became obsolete. Gates and Allen closed the doors. They had failed.

"The greatest thing in life is experience. Even mistakes have value."

In 1899, Henry Ford had a dream. In pursuit of that dream, he left his long-term, comfortable job with $150,000 in investor dollars and established the Detroit Automobile Company. In just more than a year, his fledgling auto company went bankrupt—and with it, he lost the investment.

Somehow his investors still had faith in Ford. In 1901, they invested in his next venture, the Henry Ford Company. Sadly, it went bankrupt as well.

Think about that. If you lost all of your investors' money, not once but twice, would you dare try a third time? Most wouldn't. But most aren't Henry Ford, who maintained, "Failure is simply the opportunity to begin again, this time more intelligently." And that's exactly what he did, establishing the Ford Motor Company in 1903. Five years later the company became a success with the release of the Model T.

Today, Ford is the second-largest U.S.-based automaker and the fifth largest in the world.

To the pair, *failure* was a four-letter word. The two college dropouts started looking for another opportunity and found it in a *Popular Electronics* magazine that touted a new computer system. That sparked an idea: what if they could figure out how to implement BASIC programming language for the system? Over the next eight weeks, they put their all into the challenge, and Microsoft was born (originally Micro-Soft, it combined the words *microcomputer* and *software*).

When they moved the company from Albuquerque, New Mexico, to Bellevue, Washington, they had thirteen employees and modest revenues. This year the company will exceed $86 billion in revenues, with close to 130,000 employees worldwide. No one would argue that plan B far exceeded the potential of that initial failure.

Then there's Rowland Hussey Macy. Over a twelve-year period, he opened four successive retail dry-goods stores, including the original Macy's store in downtown Haverhill, Massachusetts. All four failed. Macy thought about what he'd done with each store, determined to learn from his mistakes instead of simply giving up. In October 1858, at the age of thirty-six—old at the time for starting a new venture—he established a new dry-goods store on the corner of Sixth Avenue and Fourteenth Street in New York City, significantly north of the other dry-goods stores of the day.

As his store expanded, he stayed on top of efforts to set it apart from the competition. He used illuminated window displays to attract customers, set up themed exhibits, offered a money-back guarantee, and employed publicity stunts—including the now-famous store Santa Claus. With that, Macy's—one of the largest department-store chains in the world—was born. The red star that is the store's logo comes from a red star that was tattooed on Macy's hand when as an eighteen-year-old he worked on the whaling ship *Emily Morgan.*

And no discussion of visionary business leaders who overcame failure would be complete without Walt Disney, creator of what is arguably the happiest place on earth. Like so many of the others we've talked about, things didn't start out well for Walt Disney. His career began on a rough note when he was fired by a newspaper editor because, get this, he "lacked imagination and had no good ideas." (I'm betting the more than 600 million kids and grownups who have visited Disneyland since it opened would take issue with that embarrassing statement.)

Needing something to bring in a paycheck, Disney opened an animation studio in 1921. In near lightning speed, it went bankrupt. Forget the paycheck; after its failure, Walt Disney subsisted on dog food to survive.

If you'd had an animation company fail and had been forced to eat dog food as a result, would you dive right back into the fray with another animation company? I don't think so! But Disney did. In fact, he did it three or four more times, suffering three or four more failures until he finally got one to work. Some of the failures he suffered during those years boggle the mind. One of his early characters—Oswald the Rabbit—was stolen by Universal Studios. And they didn't stop with the rabbit; they managed to steal

Disney's entire design team. And his concept of Mickey Mouse? It was turned down outright by MGM, who warned him that a giant mouse on screen would terrify women.

Of those years, Disney reminded us, "Everyone falls down. Getting up is how you learn to walk." And reflecting on his experiences, he said, "I think it's important to have a good hard failure when you're young. I learned a lot out of that. Because it makes you kind of aware of what can happen to you. Because of it I've never had any fear in my whole life when we've been near collapse and all of that. I've never been afraid. I've never had the feeling I couldn't walk out and get a job doing something."

Consider yourself lucky if you've experienced failure. The knowledge and growth attained as a result prepares you for future endeavors.

Failure Provides Perspective

One of the great things about failure is that it helps provide perspective.

Under normal circumstances, it can be difficult to step back and gain perspective. To understand how vastly different perspective can be, consider this: a piece of bread, which seems relatively small to you, would seem enormous to an ant. But seen from outer space, something you can hold in your hand and smear with peanut butter—something that would completely crush an entire gaggle of ants—would be so small it wouldn't even register on the radar.

Your *perspective* is informed by a collection of your opinions, beliefs, and experiences. Failure—taken as part of your experience—forces you to step back and look at things in a different way. Maybe you've always looked at failure as a weakness. A mistake. A negative. Something to be avoided at all costs. And until your experience tells you otherwise, that is the perspective to which you will stubbornly cling.

Once you *experience* failure, however, and learn that it can actually be a benefit—learn that it won't actually kill you or cause irreparable damage—you find you no longer have to dread failure. You have a new perspective. A new vision. No one sets out to fail, of course—no one goes looking for failure in all the wrong places. But sometimes it happens. For some, it even happens a lot. But if you succeed in changing your perspective, you'll be prepared for that eventuality. It will no longer terrify you.

Perspective reminds us of an important principle: the world is relative, and it needs relative solutions. What works beautifully in one situation may completely collapse in another. That's where failure can creep in. But because you understand it's all relative, you can more easily pick yourself up and keep trying, knowing that just down the road is the solution that *will* work. You just have to maintain your forward momentum, and you'll get there.

With its ability to change your perspective, failure forces you to break with the norm and do something different—to think bigger. To break through the bounds you've always felt constrained by. To see a broader, grander, more inspired vision. To become a greater version of yourself, one free of old limitations. The changed perspective that comes with failure helps you focus on *trying*, not on what might happen if you try and *fail*. NBA great Michael Jordan put it this way: "I can accept failure; everyone fails at something. But I can't accept not trying."

"By All Means, Paint"

Vincent van Gogh, the brilliant Dutch Post-Impressionist painter, is among the most famous and influential figures in the history of Western art. Yet he sold only one painting—"The Red Vineyard"—in his life, and that was just months before he died.

Even though his lack of sales strained his financial and emotional well-being to its limit, he somehow managed to keep a good perspective on his art. "If you hear a voice within you say 'you cannot paint,'" he famously advised others, "by all means paint, and that voice will be silenced."

Some of the more famous works he left behind include Starry Night, Irises, Café Terrace at Night, and a haunting self-portrait. His magnificent perspective was made clear when he said, "I don't know anything with certainty, but seeing the stars makes me dream."

Jordan, a legend on the court, knows a lot about failing—and he has experienced the way it can change perspective. If you can believe it, Michael Jordan initially failed to make his high school basketball team. (Can you imagine someone with *that* talent playing for *your* school?) Once he finally got a chance to play, he was cut from the team. It was total heartbreak. And that wasn't the last of the failures he experienced.

But when you mention the name *Michael Jordan*, most people think only of success. Success may certainly be the title of the greatest basketball player in the history of the game. But even with that accolade, Jordan says, his perspective stays grounded. "I have missed more than nine thousand shots in my career. I have lost almost three hundred games. On twenty-six occasions, I have been entrusted to take the game-winning shot, and I missed. I have failed over and over and over again in my life. And that is why I succeed."

Michael Jordan personifies a healthy perspective born of failure—one that has launched him to tremendous success.

When we consider perspective, few groups understand it better than writers and artists. What seems solid, even profound, one minute can wither the next under the analytical eye of a critic. And few people suffer rejection like writers and artists—even the really good ones. Rejections are so typical, in fact, that many now-successful writers consider their early rejections badges of honor.

Look at Stephen King. His first book, *Carrie*, was rejected at least thirty times—he lost count. He got so frustrated, in fact, that he threw it away. And there it would have stayed had not his wife,

Tabitha, found the manuscript in the trash and rescued it. With renewed perspective born of his wife's encouragement, King set out to try again—and the book was accepted by Doubleday. Not only did it become a best-selling novel, it gained traction as one of the most popular horror movies ever to hit the screen. Those original thirty (at least!) failures continued to give King valued perspective—and his novels have since sold more than 350 million copies.

He's not the only one who resorted to the trash only to be rescued by a wife with keener perspective. Positivity guru Norman Vincent Peale tried repeatedly to get published but became so discouraged by rejections that he too threw his first manuscript in the trash. His wife found it there, pulled it out, and sent it to one more publisher, Simon & Schuster. *The Power of Positive Thinking* stayed on the *New York Times* best-seller list for 186 consecutive weeks, has sold more than 20 million copies, and has been translated into fifteen languages.

Possibly the most astonishing failure/rejection story of all is that of J. K. Rowling. You've heard the tale: a single mother living on welfare, she started writing *Harry Potter and the Sorcerer's Stone* on napkins in a corner café while she tended to her small daughter. Her book was rejected twelve times—once by a myopic publisher who advised that she not "quit her day job."

Seems that publisher had it all wrong, but Rowling had the perspective to keep going despite the blistering criticism. Today she is internationally renowned for her Harry Potter children's fantasy series and has sold hundreds of millions of copies that have been adapted into a blockbuster film franchise. In 2004, she became the first billionaire author. I'm guessing she doesn't miss that "day job"—you know, the one she never had to begin with.

Consider This: There's a "Right" Way to Fail

Face it: no one goes out looking for failure.

In fact, failure usually flies right at you out of nowhere and slaps you in the face, the *last* thing you were expecting. So how on earth can there be a "right" way to do something you weren't even thinking about doing?

The "right" way to fail doesn't mean you're anticipating it or that you're hunkered down waiting for it to launch a blitz. It doesn't mean you check off items on a list just so you can cover all the bases. It *does* mean you do everything you can to minimize its impact if it does come along and ambush you. And that all boils down to risk.

If you want to emerge from failure with the tenacity and ability to gather up the pieces and move on to a better future, make sure you are being wise about the risks you take, both professionally and personally. It can be a delicate balancing act because you need to risk enough to embrace change and adventure—but not so much that you risk making a devastating mistake.

In most cases, that's not as hard as it sounds. After all, as human beings, we are instinctively programmed to avoid risks that will kill us. There's a *reason* you would never throw your arms out to your sides with careless abandon and jump off a cliff at Dead Horse Point. You would eventually hit the ground, but it would be your last act in mortality. Everything that combines to make you who you are would keep you from doing something so foolish. It would be too great a risk.

What your mind and body and spirit *will* risk are ways in which you can hit the ground, then get back up. Again, and again, and again. Those are calculated risks—intelligent risks. R. H. Macy fell down three or four times while trying to make a success of his dry-goods stores. Then he took a calculated risk: he located his store far north of the competition and offered things they didn't. It worked. His days of falling down and getting back up were over.

Let's say you've experienced a failure. Let's say you've picked yourself up. Let's say you've dusted yourself off and you're determined to keep going. That's exactly as it should be. But when you're deciding what to do and where to go from here, do a few calculations. Avoid the temptation to run by the seat of your pants; instead, take a few deep breaths and come up with a couple of plans. There's nothing wrong with gut instinct as long as you've fed your gut some information. In other words, consider the possible—as well as the likely—outcomes of each plan before you jump in with both feet.

Be realistic about what you're risking. It's generally not a good idea to risk everything unless you know you have access to the resources you'll need to recover afterward *just in case* things don't work. A man I know was offered a lucrative six-month contract to work as a security engineer in Louisville, Kentucky, after a prolonged period of unemployment. Taking the contract would necessitate a move from Phoenix, Arizona. It was a risk. There was a chance the six-month contract would become permanent if they liked him and all the stars aligned, but there was also a chance the job would end after six months—and he'd be unemployed again.

He drafted several plans and, after assessing the possible outcomes, he settled on one. He took a calculated risk, loaded the essentials into his car, and drove to Kentucky. But he kept the lease on his apartment in Phoenix, renting it to an acquaintance for the six months he *knew* he'd be in Kentucky. What if the contract didn't become permanent and he was out of work again in six months? He still had a home to which he could return. What if the contract *did* become permanent? He could make a quick trip west and settle his affairs there. Neither scenario equated to jumping off the cliff at Dead Horse Point.

Try to hedge your bets—take risks, but take manageable risks. Keep moving. Keep trying. But go at a pace that challenges you without annihilating you. There's a big difference between getting a few bumps and bruises from a failure and crashing so hard you break every bone in your body.

When you *do* sustain those bumps and bruises, take careful note of what happened and how you might do things differently the next time. Then get up, get moving, and make sure there *is* a next time—because the next time could make all the difference. Chemical magnate and philanthropist Jon Huntsman Sr. put it this way: "Never quit believing that you can develop in life. Never give up. Don't deny the inward spirit that provides the drive to accomplish great things in life."

Now that you've read this chapter, you know that the key to failing the "right" way is to never, ever give up no matter what. President Richard M. Nixon, whose failures were front-page news on the world's stage, captured the right attitude when he said, "Never let your head hang down. Never give up and sit down and grieve. Find another way." No one alive when Nixon resigned can ever forget how he stood in front of the helicopter on the White House lawn, smiling and waving the victory sign as he prepared to board it for the last time. His failure may have been epic, but he was determined to survive.

Maintain your passion. Be determined. This won't be your last failure, so disabuse yourself of that notion right now. There will be more. At the very least, there will be obstacles. What will you do when they come? Decide *right now* that you will never throw in the towel. Decide *right now* that you will keep trying no matter what. Decide *right now* that quitting simply isn't an option—not for you, anyway.

Once you've calculated your risks and know where you're going, go with all your might. Invest your heart. Set your compass, and fix it on your destination. Decide you will do whatever it takes to get there. Work for free as a janitor in exchange for acting lessons? Absolutely. Start your own record label when all the rest have turned you away? Yes! Keep sending your manuscript to one publisher after another until one finally bites? You bet.

What it boils down to is this: the "right" way to fail is to keep on going. Keep on doing. Do what will eventually get you where you want to be, even if there are some potholes or hairpin turns or obstacles along the way to your destination. More than two thousand years ago, Aristotle nailed it when he said, "We are what we repeatedly do."

In your quest, whatever it is, take on the words of Britain's visionary prime minister, Winston Churchill: "Success is stumbling from failure to failure with no loss of enthusiasm."

At a moment in his career—actually, at a moment in his nation's history—when all seemed lost, Winston Churchill drew a line in the sand and made clear what had to be done. His words not only said what had to be done but inspired those who had to do it. The next time you are blessed with failure, borrow his sentiment as you get up to resume the fight:

> We shall go on to the end. We shall fight on the seas and oceans, we shall fight with growing confidence and growing strength in the air, we shall defend our Island, whatever the cost may be, we shall fight on the beaches, we shall fight on the landing grounds, we shall fight in the fields and in the streets, we shall fight in the hills; we shall never surrender.[20]

---

20 Alan Gopnik, "The Finest Hours: The Making of Winston Churchill," *The New Yorker,* Aug 30, 2010.

Chapter Four

Vision: The Ability to See the Invisible and Achieve the Impossible

*Make your vision so clear that
your fears become irrelevant.*

—*Anonymous*

The Bible tells us, "Where there is no vision, the people perish" (Proverbs 29:18). And there's a solid reason for that timeless counsel: without vision, a terrible thing happens—*nothing.*

One of the most important ways to reinvent adversity into something that allows you to move into a new and more meaningful life is to have vision. *Vision* is the ability to see beyond your current reality—to create and invent what doesn't yet exist and, most important, to become what you have not yet become. It is, as the chapter heading says, the ability to see the invisible—the things others can't see—and achieve the impossible. It's the capability to see a future for yourself not defined by your current struggles. It enables you to focus on the things that give your life purpose and meaning instead of the things that are, for now, throwing obstacles in your way.

Vision is the gift of knowing exactly who you are and who you can become. It is one of the most important things you can have as you move to reinvent any kind of adversity that's holding you back. As the renowned artist James Whistler said, "An artist is not paid for his labor but for his vision." Anyone can slap the paint of change on the canvas of life, but it takes a true vision to create of that effort a masterpiece that moves you forward to new realities.

Vision is what you become in life. It gives you the chance to imagine, to dream, and to fashion your life around those dreams *no matter what is going on in your life right now.* It also gives you the ability to fashion your life around the things you want instead of what others expect of you. And that is precisely how you grab adversity by the horns and force it to become the source of a new way of life.

Vision makes you consider things you have never considered; it has no boundaries, and it knows no limits. Most people are not limited by their abilities but by their lack of vision. As Helen Keller famously said, "The only thing worse than being blind is having sight but no vision." Having vision causes you to accept a whole new realm of possibilities.

Vision invites you to ask yourself, *How do I want my world to be better?* Vision then points the way to that better world; it drives and directs and focuses your energy until you have created exactly what it is you have envisioned. The first step toward creating that future for yourself is to envision it. Once you have embraced all of the passion in that vision, you will find yourself doing whatever it takes to make it come true.

If vision is so important, where on earth do you find it? That's the best part of all. Carl Jung, the father of analytical psychology, whose work influenced philosophy, religious studies, literature, and dozens of other fields, pointed right to the source: "Your vision will become clear only when you can look into your own heart." It's there inside you, right now. As Jung said, he "who looks outside, dreams; [he] who looks inside, awakens."

It's time for you to search your heart and awake to your unique vision, the one that will define your new life.

Life is a long and winding road peppered with lots of ruts and studded with lots of signs. Your vision is like a detailed map of that road, complete with signposts and landmarks that provide direction. If you were going on a road trip, you'd never consider leaving home without a good map. Otherwise you could end up anywhere—and, chances are, it would be far away from your planned destination. That's how a vision works for your life: it points the way and keeps you on the right road until you arrive. It clarifies where you are going and how you plan to get there.

It's clear by now that no one in life suffers just one adversity. If that were the case, it wouldn't be so tough. Once it was over, you could get up, dust yourself off, breathe a sigh of relief, and move on with the confidence that things would be smooth sailing from here on out. But that's just not how it works. Not for you, not for me, not for anyone. You're going to be faced with enduring plenty of adversity.

But here's the great part of that: if you let it, every adversity you face makes you stronger and better able to face the next. And with each adversity, you can be guided by a powerful vision of where you want to be, revisiting that vision and making necessary adjustments as you go. Your vision will help you hold on when the going gets rough because you will have focus and purpose. Regardless of what happens in your life—whether it's your first big adversity or your tenth or your hundredth—you will know what you are doing and why you are doing it. And nothing that comes along will be able to drive you off that path for long.

Revisiting and adjusting your vision is important. Just as adversity isn't a one-time thing, neither is creating a vision. Your vision should be dynamic, not static; it should be fluid and able to change with the things that happen in your life. That doesn't mean you constantly come up with an entirely new vision. It means you renew your vision and adapt and adjust it to the things that crop up in the road as you travel through life. No matter what comes along, though, your vision will be consistent in determining who are you are, what you want to become, and how you will get there.

Don't think your vision is only about goals, milestones, and achievements. That's only a small part of it. The larger part of your vision is defining who you want to *be*, the values that will help you get there, and the character you hope to develop along the way. It's then the art of applying those values and that character to the *things* you want to do, and that's where some adjustment and adaptation comes in.

There are a few reasons why vision is so important. As should be obvious by now, a vision gives you purpose. When you have vision about where you want to go and what you want to be, you automatically become part of something bigger; you're connected to a never-ending picture that gives you drive and determination.

A vision also gives you energy because you're actively working toward something *worth* the energy you need to invest. When you're battling adversity, you may find that your energy wanes and you don't feel like you have much of anything left to give. But when you craft a vision and begin to fulfill it, even as you battle your adversity, you are strengthened, invigorated, and empowered by the chance to take on something that's going to rejuvenate you.

Another reason why vision is so important is that it drives you to excellence. Without vision, there's not much need to figure out how you're going to reach the next big landmark or what kind of breakthrough you'll be able to make, because those things aren't part of your thinking. Instead, your thoughts are consumed with simply *surviving*—of simply staying on the road instead of finding out where that road leads. With a vision, you're constantly focused on how you're doing and the ways you can grow as you go, which brings with it fulfillment and joy.

Finally, a vision is important because it encourages you to take risks—to leap out of your comfort zone and take the path less traveled. There's no telling what incredible things you will find along that path when you leave your "comfort zone"—the one riddled with adversity—behind.

Let's look at a few people with extraordinary vision and what we can learn from them. I'd like to start by looking back—*way* back—to Alexander the Great, known by many as the man who conquered the world and the greatest military commander to have ever lived. He was clearly blessed with substantial military capabilities, but what really set him apart was his vision and foresight. He envisioned having command of a tremendous empire and, in fact, the empire he created stretched from Greece to India, the largest in history.

It's mind-boggling to consider his accomplishments. In addition to conquering the Persian Empire, among others, he was undefeated in battle and served as the king of all Macedonia, the king of all Greek nations, the shah of Persia, the pharaoh of Egypt, and the ruler of a number of other lands. He also ruled over several Greek dynasties in foreign lands and founded multiple cities, naming them after himself; the most famous of which is Alexandria, Egypt, which today boasts a population of 4.5 million. Finally, he solidified the economy of all his lands, creating a single currency, and unified a number of Greek city states that had been warring.

And talk about vision: Alexander the Great did it all before he died at the shockingly young age of thirty-three.

Examples of extraordinary vision are easy to find in most fields of endeavor. Many associate dogged determination and having a vision with athletes, and there are many who personify those abilities. Among the top is Alex Rodriguez, once a twenty-one-year-old rookie who consistently hit home runs and was a sensational shortstop. He had grown up without a father in a New Jersey suburb, but from the time he was young he developed and fostered a vision that took him to the major leagues. In everything he did, he tenaciously worked to make that vision a reality.

In 2000, Rodriguez signed a ten-year, $250 million contract with the Texas Rangers; it was a record contract for any athlete in any sport. For most, that would have been good enough, but not for a man with Rodriguez's vision. In 2007, he exercised the opt-out clause in his contract, which freed him up to sign yet another record-breaking deal: this one with the New York Yankees for more than $300 million over ten years.

And let's consider Scott Boras, the man who negotiated those two record-breaking baseball contracts for Alex Rodriguez. From the time he was young, Boras loved baseball but knew he didn't have the native talent to excel in the game. Instead, he got a law degree and tenaciously pursued his vision of being a successful agent for the men who did play baseball.

That vision became reality, and not just because of Alex Rodriguez. Today, Boras is the most aggressive and successful sports agent of all time in any sport. Jerry Crasnick, author of *License to Deal*, estimates that Boras has negotiated more than $1 billion in contracts and endorsement deals for the baseball players he represents. Because of his remarkable success, Boras has been offered even more profitable deals from other sports stars and even Hollywood actors, but he has turned them down, preferring to remain true to his vision of a lifetime of participation in baseball.

Mark Cuban didn't have the easiest start in life. He grew up in a Jewish working-class family in a Pittsburgh suburb where his father upholstered automobiles for a living. When Cuban wanted a pair of expensive basketball sneakers, he had to earn them by selling trash bags to raise the money. That experience sparked in Cuban a vision of business success, and he set out with steely resolve to make the vision a reality. One success led to another until he founded and ran the internet company whose sale enabled him to buy the NBA's Dallas Mavericks. At the age of forty-nine, he became a billionaire in fulfillment of his aggressive vision. Today, in addition to his gig with the Mavericks, he is a founding owner of the HDNet cable network.

Let's consider a handful of people in the performing arts. When Jim Carrey was fifteen, he had to drop out of school to help support his family—who was by then living in a van. He had always dreamed of being a comedian but knew the traditional channels were no longer open to him. Instead of changing his dream, he changed his approach, having his father drive him to comedy clubs all over Toronto. To stay motivated during those difficult times, he adopted a powerful vision. He wrote himself a check for $10 million for "acting services rendered" and dated the check for 1994. Carrey kept the check in his wallet and looked at it every day for inspiration and to remind himself of his vision.

From that humble beginning, he became known as one of the best comedic actors of his era. In fact, remember that check? In 1994, he learned he would earn *exactly* $10 million for his role in *Dumb and Dumber.*

As a young athlete, Arnold Schwarzenegger swore by the power of visualization to reach his bodybuilding goals. He had, he said, a vision of eventually developing a body like that of Reg Park, a British bodybuilder who won the title of Mr. Universe three different times. That body, Schwarzenegger said, "was there in my mind; I only had to grow enough to fill it. The more I focused in on this image and worked and grew, the more I saw it was real and possible for me to be like him."

Remember what I said about having to revisit and adapt your vision? That's exactly what Schwarzenegger had to do when he switched from an athletic career to one of acting and politics. The career focus was different, but the process of building a vision and working to make it a reality remained the same. "What you do is create a vision of who you want to be," he said, "an then live that picture as if it were already true."

Award-winning actor Will Smith developed a powerful vision for himself as a teen, but it didn't involve going to college. Instead, he wanted to be a rapper. Before long, he reinvented that vision, determined to become a highly sought-after actor along with his musical involvement. Using visualization techniques to help him throughout his journey, he said, "In my mind, I've always been an A-list Hollywood superstar. Y'all just didn't know yet."

Smith says that one of the things that guided his efforts and his vision was a well-known quote from Confucius: "He who says he can and he who says he can't are both usually right." Smith determined he could—and, boy, was he right.

In the music arena, Smith has won four Grammy Awards and has been nominated for four more. He has also won five MTV Video Music Awards and garnered a number of other awards. To date, he has starred in twenty-eight films, and he has been nominated for two Academy Awards and five Golden Globe Awards. He is also the winner of a prestigious Hollywood Film Award, as well as a number of other prominent honors. In April 2007, *Newsweek* called Smith "the most powerful actor in Hollywood."

And how about a name that keeps coming up as an example of people who have overcome adversity? Oprah Winfrey. It turns out she's also an incredible example of someone who developed an impressive vision for herself. As a child, she watched her grandmother toil relentlessly at backbreaking work to make ends meet. Seeing that happen, she told herself repeatedly, "My life won't be like this. My life won't be like this. It will be better."

Winfrey eventually formulated the vision that guided her life, and with it she pulled herself out of poverty and has become one of the wealthiest women in the world. She is also one of the world's greatest advocates of creating and living by a vision. She has frequently discussed the power of having a vision on her television show and in the pages of her magazine, and she has taught others how to create vision boards to help realize their dreams. When it comes to vision, she tells people, "Create the highest, grandest vision possible for your life, because you become what you believe."

Author Ayn Rand is one of the most profound examples of creating and following a vision. She grew up in tsarist Russia and saw her father's successful pharmacy confiscated by the invading Bolsheviks; as a result, her family had to flee the country. Rand despised the totalitarian environment to which she'd been subjected, so at twenty-one she harnessed all her courage and came to the United States on a student visa. She had a vision that seemed improbable to everyone else, but it guided her life: she wanted to make a name for herself as a Hollywood writer.

Against all odds and despite a considerable number of naysayers, she made it. But after writing several plays, it was time for Rand to adjust her vision: she realized her real talent was in fiction writing, and that's where she focused her efforts. Once more, she made it despite all the people who said a poor Russian immigrant didn't have a prayer.

Now recognized as one of the most influential fiction writers of all time, she's penned such enduring best sellers as *The Fountainhead* and *Atlas Shrugged*. A survey conducted by the Library of Congress found that readers ranked *Atlas Shrugged* as the second most influential book in their lives, second only to the Bible.

Talk about vision—I'd like to share with you the story of a man who had incredible vision for himself and who now dedicates himself to helping others develop and carry out their own visions. He is now known as America's number-one success coach, but it wasn't always that way, and the story of how he achieved that title is nothing less than miraculous.

Jack Canfield earned a bachelor of arts degree from Harvard University and a master's in psychological education from the University of Massachusetts. His studies focused on what made successful people different, and he concentrated on figuring out what motivated them, what drove them, and what inspired them.

One of the earliest champions of what has become known as "peak performance," he developed a series of specific methods and results-oriented activities to help people take on greater challenges and produce breakthrough results. Armed with what he had learned, he went on the speaking circuit, where he shared his insights with audiences around the world as well as with media, universities, and professional organizations.

In 1992, Canfield decided to compile the "inspiring, healing, motivational, and transformational" stories he told on the speaking circuit in a book that would "open the heart and rekindle the spirit."[21] He enlisted the help of promoter and salesman Mark Victor Hansen. Together they decided on 101 stories, penned the chapters, and chose a title (Canfield says the words *Chicken Soup* appeared to him in a dream in which the hand of God scrawled them across a chalkboard[22]). They then found an agent and flew to New York to meet with publishers.

Things didn't go well in New York. Publishers snubbed the stories as "too nicey-nice." In order to take a risk on the book,

21 Katy Waldman, "Happiness, Inspiration, and Wellness: The Ingredients of *Chicken Soup for the Soul*," *The Slate Book Review*, November 7, 2014.
22 Ibid.

publishers needed to believe it would sell at least twenty thousand copies, and not one felt it had even a remote chance of doing *that*. At the end of the day, Canfield and Hansen received 144 rejections from what seemed to be every major publisher in America. At that point, most authors would have retreated with their tails between their legs, but not Jack Canfield. He had a vision for his book, and he was determined to see it through.

As so often happens with a vision, Canfield had to adapt—make adjustments, change direction, all while keeping the end goal in mind. So he and Hansen started putting "commitment to buy" forms on the chairs at every motivational conference at which Canfield spoke. Those forms started to stack up, and they finally had more than twenty thousand promises to buy the book. That was enough to persuade Peter Vegso at Florida's HCI publishing house to take a risk, and the first *Chicken Soup for the Soul* was published in the summer of 1993.

The rest is history—and powerfully demonstrates the strength of a vision. There are now more than 250 titles in the Chicken Soup for the Soul series; the books have been translated into forty-three languages, have been published in more than a hundred countries, and have sold more than 500 million copies worldwide. Chicken Soup for the Soul is one of the best-known brands in the world; according to a Harris Poll, 88.7 percent of all Americans recognize it. It's a multimillion-dollar franchise that even includes an auxiliary line of pet food.

And what of Jack Canfield, who could have easily given up after even a few dozen of those 144 rejections? He now holds the Guinness Book World Record for having seven books simultaneously on the *New York Times* best-seller list. He also hold the Guinness Book World Record for the largest book signing ever (for *Chicken Soup for the Kid's Soul*). And he is the only author to win both the ABBY (American Booksellers Book of the Year) and Southern California Book Publicist Awards in the same year.

He has also been a featured guest on more than a thousand radio and television programs in nearly every major market in the world. They include, among others, *Larry King Live*, *Oprah*, the *Today Show*, the *CBS Evening News*, the *NBC Nightly News*, *Montel*, *Inside Edition*, *20/20*, *Eye to Eye*, and *Fox and Friends*. He also has five weekly columns syndicated to newspapers by King Features, a blog network with more than 9.5 million monthly unique visitors, and is featured on a radio network for more than two hundred radio stations covering more than 65 percent of the United States.

This, then, is a man who knows firsthand about vision and how to execute it. And he has shared part of that knowledge by advising people to create a vision book or vision board—powerful techniques from which I have personally benefitted. I'd like to recommend them to you as a way to reinvent your adversity because I know how amazing the results can be. As Jack Canfield himself writes, "Your brain will work tirelessly to achieve the statements you give your subconscious mind.

And when those statements are the affirmations and images of your goals, you are destined to achieve them!"[23]

Let's start with the vision book.[24] Canfield describes it as "one of the most valuable visualization tools available to you," your image of the future—"a tangible representation of where you are going. It represents your dreams, your goals, and your ideal life." Representing your vision with images and pictures, he says, actually strengthens and stimulates your emotions and helps you achieve the things you desire.

Once you've defined your vision, it's time to illustrate it visually. The process is really quite simple: get a book, and fill it with things that inspire you and pertain to your vision: photographs, magazine cutouts, inspirational words, pictures from the internet, quotations, thoughts, and anything else that inspires you. Canfield also recommends putting a happy picture of yourself in the book. Finally, he says, write down the date you created your book.

There's one caveat: Canfield advises you be selective in what you include and that you avoid chaos and clutter, since "you don't want to attract chaos into your life." He suggests using "only the words and images that best represent your purpose, your ideal future, and words that inspire positive emotions in you. There is

23 "How to Create an Empowering Vision Board," published on LinkedIn and StumbleUponFacebook, can be accessed at http://www.getmotivation.com/motivation-blog/2012/06/how-to-create-an-empowering-vision-board-by-jack-canfield/.
24 The following information on how to create a vision book is from Jack Canfield's blog, "How to Create an Empowering Vision Board."

beauty in simplicity and clarity. Too many images and too much information will be distracting and harder to focus on."

If you have a vision for several areas of your life, you may want to create more than one vision book. For example, you may have separate vision books for personal goals, career goals, and financial goals.

Canfield suggests you keep your book on your nightstand next to your bed and spend time reviewing it every morning and evening. During these times, you should visualize, affirm, believe, and internalize your goals.

"The time you spend visualizing in the evening just before bed is especially powerful," he writes. "The thoughts and images that are present in your mind during the last forty-five minutes before going to sleep are the ones that will replay themselves repeatedly in your subconscious mind throughout the night, and the thoughts and images that you begin each day with will help you to create a vibrational match for the future you desire."

Canfield suggests feeling the inspiration your book offers, holding it in your hands and really visualizing what it represents, reading the inspirational words aloud, believing that future is already yours, and really *feeling* yourself in that life. Along with these things, he says, you should be grateful for the good already in your life, acknowledge the changes you have already seen and felt, and acknowledge the presence of God in your life.

You shouldn't remove the pictures or images that represent goals you achieve. Those should stay in your book as powerful reminders of what you've already accomplished—and effective reminders of your capabilities. "Much like a time capsule, this book will document your personal journey, your dreams, and your achievements for that particular year," Canfield writes. "It will become a record of your growth, awareness, and expansion that you will want to keep and reflect back upon in years to come. . . . Your Vision Book is meant to be kept and cherished."

It's a good idea, he says, to create a new vision book each year. "As you continue to grow, evolve and expand, your dreams will too," he writes. "Your Vision Book[s] . . . chronicle not only your dreams, but your growth and achievements."

Creating of a vision board[25] is similar, but you post the images and words on a board instead of in a book. You can use a bulletin board, poster board, or even a wall. In addition to posting images, consider posting inspiring quotes and words that describe how you want to feel, such as *courage, love,* or *imagination.* As with the vision book, Canfield suggests creating a new vision board every year.

Keep your board where you will see it every day, such as near your bed, in your kitchen, or near your desk. "By putting a vision board somewhere you can see every day, you will prompt yourself to visualize your ideal life on a regular basis," Canfield writes. "And that's important because visualization activates the creative powers of your subconscious mind and programs your brain to notice available resources that were always there, but escaped your notice."

---

25 Information on the vision board is from Jack Canfield's blog, found at http://www.cs.mun.ca/~ingrid/CUPEPounds/HowTo.pdf., and from Jack Canfield, "21 Ways to Make Your Vision Board More Powerful," Vision_Board_Checklist_Jack_Canfield.pdf, available from Jack Canfield.

Having a vision board where you can see it every day, he writes, will help you "naturally become more motivated to reach your goals. You'll start to unexpectedly do things that move you closer to your ideal life."

As you make either a vision book or vision board, Canfield gives an important warning: "Although a daily practice of visualization is vital, you don't need to spend all day thinking about your goals for this technique to work," he writes. "In fact, spending too much time in visualization can rob you of something essential— living in the moment."

Whether you choose to create a vision book or vision board, read the words aloud and close your eyes after each one, creating a visual image of the completed goal, adding the emotions and physical sensations you would be feeling if you had already experienced it. If you can, add sounds, smells, and tastes to make it even more real. Canfield suggests that once you've finished your visualizing, release it and spend the rest of your day in the present.

There are many examples of athletes who have harnessed the power of vision to help them compete, but one of the most compelling is Lindsey Vonn, who took gold in downhill skiing and is one of only four female skiers to win four World Cup overall championships. She believes her ability to visualize is what has brought her almost countless victories in competition.

"I always visualize the run before I do it," she says. "By the time I get to the start gate, I've run that race 100 times already in my head, picturing how I'll take the turns." But that's not all: she also adds physical "vision" to her imaginary runs, shifting her weight back and forth as if she were literally on skis. She also practices the specific breathing patterns she expects to use during the race.

The power of her vision is intense; once she visualizes the course, she never forgets it. During the actual race, she goes through "exactly the run that I want to have," a system that has led to repeated success.

Leaders in industry have also been known as great visionaries. Sam Walton is known today as the farsighted entrepreneur behind Walmart, an industry that never would have happened without his persistent vision. Asked about his success, Walton once said, "High expectations are the key to everything." And it was Walton's expectations—his unique vision—that launched an empire.

After graduating college, Walton got his first job in retail with JCPenney, which at that time was still a relatively small company. He liked retail business, though, and when he returned to private life after serving as an army captain in an intelligence unit in World War II, he decided he wanted to make retail his career. Using a $25,000 loan from his father-in-law, he bought a Ben Franklin franchise in Newport, Arkansas.

Working with his younger brother, James, Walton managed to expand his franchise to fifteen Ben Franklin stores in the next two decades. But Walton was frustrated: he had a vision of taking his stores into rural communities, and the owners of Ben Franklin aggressively resisted his efforts. He also had a powerful vision of radically cutting costs, something else he was unable to do under the Ben Franklin owners. Dedicated to his two-part vision, he summoned the courage to walk away from Ben Franklin and strike out on his own.

Walton opened his first Walmart store in Rogers, Arkansas, in 1962. His vision proved to be exactly what consumers were looking for, and his success was swift. Within just four years, his new chain included up to twenty stores and continued to grow. With every step in his expansion, he vowed to remake the retail industry in line with his vision of cutting costs and taking his stores to rural markets.

One of the ways he made things work was to focus on logistics. Though his stores were located in rural regions, they were never more than a day's drive away from a Walmart regional warehouse. Not only that, but he distributed merchandise with his own trucking service and bought all merchandise in volume so he could offer lower prices to customers.

Walton knew he had to do whatever it took to stay true to that vision. He often started his work day at 4:30 a.m. and expected results from all who worked for him. A key to his unbridled success was that while he never lost sight of his original vision, he wasn't afraid to change course or shuffle things if he didn't like what was happening. He also did something others hadn't yet tried: according to *Time*, Walton "may have been the first true information-aged CEO." He was the first to hire a computer specialist to completely overhaul the company's inventory system and logistics—and the resulting efficiency enabled Walmart to outcompete pretty much every other department store in existence.

In 1991, Walmart surpassed Sears, Roebuck and Company as the nation's largest retailer; its stock worth had skyrocketed to $45 billion, and even in the grips of a severe economic downturn, Walmart's sales increased by more than 40 percent. Through it all, Walton firmly executed his original vision of radical cost cutting and expansion to rural areas.

In 1992, Walton was inducted into the Junior Achievement U.S. Business Hall of Fame. In March of that year, he received the Presidential Medal of Freedom from President George H. W. Bush. And in 1998, he was included on *Time*'s list of the one hundred most influential people of the twentieth century. The business college at the University of Arkansas—the Sam M. Walton College of Business—is named in his honor.

Today, Walmart Stores, Inc., also runs Sam's Club warehouse stores. Walmart now operates in the United States as well as in more than fifteen international markets.

A number of prophetic thinkers hailed for their leadership achieved the success they did because of their farseeing vision. Henry Ford had a vision of being able to mass-produce automobiles, something that had never been attempted. He started Ford Motor Company with virtually none of his own money, raising funds from friends for his initial working capital and negotiating deals with suppliers, which enabled him to purchase parts on credit. Staying true to his vision, he became the first to successfully mass-produce automobiles and is famous for pioneering the assembly line.

John Rockefeller had a vision of making oil available at lower prices, something no one in the industry believed was possible. But no one could dissuade Rockefeller or cause him to abandon his vision. He knew he had to start from the ground floor, so he scrimped and saved to buy his first oil refinery in 1862. By the 1870s, he had become a dominant force in the industry, offering discounts to railroads who agreed to carry his oil across the country. That in turn enabled him to sell his oil to customers at previously unheard-of low prices.

Carrying out his vision of reducing the cost of oil across the market, Rockefeller became one of America's earliest business heroes, still celebrated for his "ability to refine crude oil to produce kerosene and other products better, cheaper, and in greater quantity than anyone thought possible."

What Rockefeller did for oil, Andrew Carnegie did for steel. Still regarded as the "king of steel," Carnegie was working as a telegrapher in the 1850s when he developed his vision of producing steel at affordable prices in a way that would revolutionize the industry. And that's exactly what happened. He started by getting a better-paying job as a bond salesman, and in the 1860s, he started investing in railroads, bridges, and oil derricks, all "ingredients" that would lead to his founding of U. S. Steel. By the 1890s, tenaciously sticking to his vision, U.S. Steel became the "largest and most profitable industrial enterprise in the world," and Carnegie was the second-wealthiest man in history. In 1901, having fulfilled his vision of five decades earlier, he sold his company to J. P. Morgan.

Like Carnegie, Thomas Edison got his start as a telegraph operator—and like Carnegie, Edison had a vision for a better world. At the time, the only available lighting was sunlight during the day and gas-powered lamps after the sun went down. Edison believed there had to be a better way, and he focused on that vision. Not only did he invent the electric light bulb (after more than a thousand hiccups), he is one of two who invented the modern electrical grid (the other was Nikola Tesla). The impact of Edison's vision has been staggering. According to the *Objective Standard*, "within fifty years of Edison introducing the electric grid, gas light was all but forgotten, and electricity emerged as the power source for the masses."

And no one can forget Nelson Mandela and his vision for an equal and free future for all citizens of his country regardless of the color of their skin. It was a vision that was not popular, at least not among the people who were in power, yet he doggedly pursued it, refusing to give up.

Once the National Party gained power in South Africa in 1948, the all-white government immediately began enforcing policies of racial segregation under a system of legislation it called apartheid. Though some racial segregation had existed for centuries in South Africa, under the policies of apartheid, that segregation became much more strict and systematic; people were clearly divided along racial lines, and those who were white were considered superior. It was a system Mandela could not tolerate for himself or for his race.

He never abandoned his vision, though his efforts brought him great personal adversity. As mentioned previously, he was even put in prison for his work, serving thirty years at hard labor for the vision he refused to abandon. Finally released from prison, he continued with the same focus and determination, eventually becoming the first black president of South Africa, ending the nation's policy of apartheid and ensuring all citizens of his country a free and equal future.

We owe much of our technological acumen to a handful of people with a vision for bettering the way we work. Steve Jobs, who left college with nothing more than the overwhelming feeling that he couldn't find his true calling there, had a vision of everyone eventually having a personal computer. In order to make things work, Jobs had to sell his Volkswagen van; his partner, Steve Wozniak, had to sell his most prized possession, his HP scientific calculator. Together they managed to raise the $1,300 needed to develop their first prototype in Jobs's tiny garage. Their innovative work led to the line of Apple products we now enjoy—including, of course, the personal computer. Jobs later founded Pixar, the animated movie giant, and returned to Apple to lead the creation of the iPod.

Another success story that started out in a garage was that of William Hewlett and David Packard, who also had a vision of making electronic products and semiconductors available to everyone who wanted them. In 1939, they managed to scrape together $538, and they never looked back. With patience and determination, they worked to make their vision a reality. Today, HP is a household name. Indeed, there are few households in America that do not have at least one of the products that resulted from the pair's innovative vision.

With a vision that there had to be a better way to access the incomprehensible amount of information available on the internet, Sergey Brin and Larry Page—two Stanford PhD candidates—went to work to make that happen. Conspiring in their dorm room, the pair managed to convince Sun cofounder Andy Bechtolsheim that their vision had merit, and Bechtolsheim wrote them a check for $100,000. The result of their vision and dedicated work, Google, "rewrote the rules of business and transformed our culture," wrote Wired.com editor John Battelle.

A similar vision led Stanford University students Jerry Yang and David Filo to develop a web portal for their personal use after they had difficulty finding information on their university's network. The web crawler they created from that simple vision had the ability to track down what they needed and make the network easily searchable. Expanding their vision to the wider internet, the pair came up with Yahoo!, which has become one of the world's top search engines and boasts $7 billion in revenue.

It's clear people with vision have the potential to change not only their own lives but the lives of countless others. Nelson Mandela stuck with his vision of abolishing apartheid and changed the future of every black person in South Africa. John Rockefeller believed oil could be sold at a much lower price, and his efforts revolutionized an industry. Steve Jobs had a vision that transformed computers from the ungainly mainframes that filled an entire room to laptops and iPods everyone could use. And the visions of a couple of innovative students gave the world a search engine that puts information at our fingertips.

These visionaries all had a few things in common. They were optimistic about the future and refused to give up, even when others told them they were crazy. They were obsessive about making tomorrow better than today. They refused to settle for the status quo. They drew others into their vision. They refused to be satisfied and instead were fueled with great hope for what could be. And no matter what was happening around them, they held on to the vision that filled their souls.

These are the qualities you need if you hope to reinvent your adversity into something life-changing. You need to believe in your future—that it holds something better for you than what you're enduring right now. You need a clear and concise vision about what you want that future to *be*. And you need to be willing to execute that vision. And here's the key to that: your vision has to be so clear, so real, that you can describe it in painstaking detail. Only then will you be able to execute it.

That's your important first step.

What? All that work to come up with a vision is *only a first step*?

Yes. Because then you need to have a plan about *how* you're going to execute your vision. Without a plan, your vision will stay exactly where it is right now: in your mind. It's especially important if you need someone else to help you—if you expect someone else to be part of executing your vision. Steve Jobs had Steve Wozniak, a guy who was willing to sell his prized scientific calculator so the two could start building their prototype. Had Jobs not been able to describe his vision with passion and to the most minute detail, there's no way Wozniak would have parted with that calculator. Jobs had to have enough passion about that vision it was virtually contagious. Lucky for all of us, he did.

One of the surest ways to reinvent your adversity into something that will transform your life is with a vision—and there are four basic steps to making that work. First, of course, you must decide on your vision. Your vision is something only *you* can decide on. Your mother can't tell you what it is. Your spouse can't tell you what it is. Your best friend can't tell you what it is. *You* have to figure it out. You're going to be seeing it, hearing it, breathing it, living it for what may be a number of years, so you'd better settle on something that fills you with passion and makes you want to get up in the morning.

Next, you have to be completely clear on what your vision is. You have to be able to describe it down to the slightest detail. This isn't the step where you make plans; instead, this is the step where you think about every single aspect of your vision and what it's going to look like when it becomes reality. It can be very helpful to write your vision down. Write about it until you think there's nothing left to describe, then keep writing.

Next, make your plan. *This* is where you figure out how you are going to execute your vision. This is where you come face-to-face with the reality of what it's going to take. This is where you come to terms with the sacrifices you're going to have to make in order to make your vision a reality. This is the Jobs and Wozniak moment: they had to clear out a space in the garage, tiny as it was, and sell the van and the scientific calculator if they hoped to be able to build that first prototype.

This third step, making your plan, can be a rough one: you're going to realize with a whole lot of clarity how little you know about what it's going to take. Don't let that deter you. Put in the work to find out what it's going to take. Do your due diligence.

By the way, you'll find an unexpected benefit from this planning step. Not only will you put into place the things you need to make your vision a reality, the very process of making a plan will help distract you from your current adversity. You will find that your thoughts, passions, and heart become occupied with something other than the problems you're having—and that in itself is a blessed relief.

The final step, of course, is to carry out your plan. When you first start out, you may be tempted to give up; it's natural to decide your plan is just a wild-eyed scheme after all and that it will never work. Stop that right now! Things will almost definitely be harder than you ever imagined, but you can do hard things. You're a survivor, and you have proven by weathering the storm of your adversity that you can do anything you put your mind to. And that includes carrying out your vision.

As you work to achieve your vision, incorporate in your life the hallmark characteristics of people with vision. Be open-minded; stay flexible. Even though you have a well-thought-out plan, be willing to change some of the details if you need to. It doesn't mean you're abandoning your vision—it means you're doing whatever is necessary to make it reality.

Be imaginative. Dream big. Don't allow others to determine what you're able to do. Harness the power of your imagination, and go where others may not dare to go. And never, ever be timid. Be brave and be daring; don't do something incredibly stupid, but be willing to take calculated risks. The risk-takers are the ones who realize the biggest rewards. Get over your fear of failure; instead, fear what might happen if you don't go for what you want. As President Franklin D. Roosevelt famously said, "We have nothing to fear but fear itself."

Maintain conviction and devotion to your vision. Sure, there are going to be risks, and there is going to be uncertainty, even if you have crafted what looks like the perfect plan. So when you encounter a few ruts in the road—or even potholes that threaten to completely swallow you—keep going. Soon those things will be in your rearview mirror and you'll find yourself that much closer to the thing you so desperately want. Remember that an obstacle is not the end; it's merely a temporary stopping point. You can push past any obstacle that presents itself if you're persistent enough and have enough resolve.

While you're at it, bring others along for the ride. Behave in a way that helps people trust you. Share your vision and your passion. Ask for help when you need it, and let others share in the joy and accomplishment that comes with realizing your vision.

And whatever else you do, continue to hope. Adversity may have you feeling you are trapped in a corner, but you *know* there is a whole wide world out there beyond what's happening right now. This adversity isn't permanent. It does not define you. It does not make decisions for you or about you. It's a temporary setback that will soon be part of your past, something that has the potential to make you stronger and wiser. Your hope will help you with all of that and will be a firm anchor when you face future setbacks.

Above all, remember these words of English author Neil Gaiman: "The one thing that you have that nobody else has is *you*. Your voice, your mind, your story, your vision. So write and draw and build and play and dance and live as only you can."

And as you start out to dream and fulfill your magnificent vision, believe with all your heart in the words of Ayn Rand:

> Throughout the centuries there were men who took first steps down new roads armed with nothing but their own vision. Their goals differed, but they all had this in common: that the step was first, the road new, the vision unborrowed, and the response they received—hatred. The great creators—the thinkers, the artists, the scientists, the inventors—stood alone against the men of their time. Every great new thought was opposed. Every great new invention was denounced. The first motor was considered foolish. The airplane was considered impossible. The power loom was considered vicious. Anesthesia was considered

sinful. But the men of unborrowed vision went ahead. They fought, they suffered and they paid. But they won.

They won, and so will you.

Chapter Five

Self-Motivation and Real Change

*Getting over a painful experience is much like
crossing monkey bars. You have to let go
at some point in order to move forward.*

—*C. S. Lewis*

If you've just come through a difficult period of adversity—
or especially if you're still in it—the thought of *change* may
be a terrifying one. Because when you're struggling with all
your might to simply maintain equilibrium, you're generally not
embracing the notion of change. Change is challenging. Change
is hard. Change demands focus and energy. Change is frightening.
And right now, you may just want to stay in bed and pull the covers
up over your head.

But please believe this: change is the best thing for you right now.
Yes, right now. *Especially* right now. Even after what you've
gone through or are still going through. As Benjamin Franklin
wrote, "When you're finished changing, you're finished." American
writer Richard Bach, author of *Jonathan Livingston Seagull*, echoed

much the same sentiment when he penned, "Here is the test to find whether your mission on earth is finished. If you're alive, it isn't."

If you're reading this, *your* mission isn't finished. And here's the good news: everything you've been through or are still going through has prepared you for what lies ahead in some very compelling ways. If you think you're not up to the task and can't muster the energy, think again. As yoga master Bikram Choudhury said, "Never too old, never too bad, never too late, never too sick to start from scratch once again." That's *you*. You're never too *anything*—beat up, exhausted, torn, battered, broke, weary, damaged—to start from scratch again. In fact, the change involved in starting over will transform your life and allow you to reinvent your adversity. As motivational coach Bob Proctor put it, "It doesn't matter where you are, you are nowhere compared to where you can go."

Before we get into all the benefits of change, though, let me hit the pause button for just a minute. Because before you can dive in and start to make the critical changes that will help you overcome adversity, there are two things you need to do. Don't worry—there are just two. This isn't rocket science, and it won't overwhelm you. But it's imperative. Ready?

First of all, figure out how *you* contributed to the adversity.

Hold on. *You* contributed to the adversity? Yes, you did. How can I say that without even knowing what you've gone through? Because it always applies. Somehow you had a part in what happened.

Your part may have been very passive, but it was still your part. Maybe you gave someone else your power. Maybe you weren't engaged in the situation. Maybe you simply didn't see the hand-writing on the wall. When I suffered a cataclysmic set of events that led to me losing my company (and pretty much everything else), I didn't *actively* do anything to cause all of that. So what *did* I do? I wasn't engaged enough to know that my CFO was keeping two sets of books and not updating the main system. I let the thing slip through my fingers because of my blind trust in someone else.

Don't get me wrong: by asking that you identify your contri-bution to the downfall, I'm not asking that you get bogged down in the trenches or wallow in guilt. I'm suggesting you ask yourself a crucial question: *What could I have done differently?* Until you figure that out, it will be tough for you to get what you need from the situation—and, as a result, tough for you to move beyond it.

There's another reason why figuring out your role is so valuable, and this one swings to the opposite end of the spectrum: until you figure out how you contributed to the adversity, you may have the mistaken impression that it was *all* you. It wasn't.

When you're stuck in the quicksand of adversity, it's easy to think it's all about you. To feel alone and abandoned. To discount the other people involved (whether directly or indirectly) and what it's doing to them. Once you try to determine what you did to cause the whole thing, you'll get a clear and accurate assessment of it all—and you will realize it involves at least one other person. And with a firm grasp on that, you'll have a much better idea on where to go from here. And as you go through that entire process, remember: you are human, and you won't always do everything right. Be gentle with yourself.

And here's the second thing you need to do: *do something now.* You've heard the old saying "Good things come to those who wait." Well, that's simply not true. At least not when it comes to adversity. You can't wait for things to resolve themselves; you need to move, and move quickly, to get beyond it all.

I have faced some pretty stiff adversity off and on from the time I was in elementary school. For a long time, I didn't even recognize it as adversity; I thought that's just the way life was. As a result, I wasn't really told how to overcome it—instead, I learned out of necessity how to adjust to it and move on with my life.

I'd like to share some of what you need to do *right now.* The first is to accept the things you cannot change. You're going to get very frustrated if you spend a whole lot of time and energy trying to change something that is out of your capacity to change. Along with that, realize that starting over is okay. Instead of focusing on what you might have to lose, start over with gusto. The visionary Steve Jobs, in addressing Stanford graduates in 2005, said, "Remembering you are going to die is the best way I know to avoid the trap of thinking you have something to lose. You are already naked. There is no reason not to follow your heart."

As you move to action, decide that you *will* control your own destiny. You want to involve the guidance and direction of God, of course, but vow right now to take charge. Prioritize. Decide what's most important, and take things one at a time. And laugh. Laugh a lot, even at yourself. Laughter is good for the soul.

As you start down the road to reinventing your adversity, don't give up if you're not successful with your first try. Remember that failure can be good (review chapter 3 if you need to). Keep trying. Hockey great Wayne Gretzky, who scored the most goals of any NHL player, famously said, "You miss 100 percent of the shots you never take." Don't let the failure to act take you completely out of the game!

Andre Gide, winner of the Nobel Prize in Literature for his sensitive examination of the human condition, sagely pointed out, "Man cannot discover new oceans unless he has the courage to lose sight of the shore." Your job *right now* is to stop clinging to the familiar—to get in that boat and row with all your might away from the shore that has swept you into riptides of adversity.

Once you've acknowledged your part in the adversity and determined to take immediate action, it's time to focus on change. As we've already established, change is hard. It's a challenge. It demands energy. And it's often slow—mind-numbingly slow. But it's also a good thing, an incredible thing to embrace as you reinvent your adversity.[26] Let's look at some of the reasons why change is such a good thing.

For one, change pushes you out of your comfort zone. You know what it's like in the comfort zone: things are easy. You can predict what's going to happen without a lot of difficulty. Even in

---

26 Ideas about the positive nature of change are adapted from Amber Rose Monaco, "5 Reasons Change Is Good for You," *Huffington Post*, April 16, 2017.

the middle of adversity, you get into a routine; it's the one that has worked most of the time to keep things on an even keel, even when the "even keel" isn't the most desirable.

Change boots you right out of that comfort zone and requires you to do something new and different. It challenges your assumptions. It tests your mindset, your opinions, and your beliefs. You are forced to find new ways of doing things and different ways of interacting with the people around you. All of this gives you a fresh perspective on what is possible and where you can be.

Along with pushing you out of your comfort zone, change helps you figure out who you really are. You probably know very clearly that the adversity you're going through isn't where you want to stay, but you may not know what else is possible until you vow to make some changes. With those changes, you'll find that your mind expands. You'll figure out what you can handle and what you can't. Knowing your limitations as well as your possibilities helps you build a better path moving forward out of adversity.

As you embrace change, you will find you are becoming more flexible and adaptable. There will still be occasional chaos in your life—but you will confront it with greater confidence that you can handle it in positive ways. You will welcome new situations because you will know you can flourish in any circumstance.

Change not only brings new circumstances but new perspectives, new experiences, and new opportunities. All of these are powerful, and all of these will teach you valuable lessons you could never have imagined. And with each new lesson learned, you'll pick up a whole array of tools that will help you meet the next adversity with know-how and capability.

I could go on. But here's the bottom line: you can read all about change from now until the end of time, but until you are inspired and motivated to do it, nothing is going to happen. And your willingness to change will come when you realize that *nothing is going to happen until you make a move.*

And when will you make a move? You will make a move when you are sick and tired of being sick and tired.

There are lots of reasons you may be hesitant to make a move to change. Maybe you don't think you have what it takes. (You do.) You may blame it on your race. Or how about this one: I wish I had a dollar for every person I've heard blame their dysfunctional family for their current miseries. News flash: you may have been temporarily imprisoned in a really rough family situation, but that doesn't have to be your life sentence. In just a minute, you'll read about some people who had unbelievably bad family situations but managed to get above it all.

I like to illustrate the decision to change with a fun analogy about a candy store. When you walk into the candy store, you find out everything in it has a price tag—just like everything in life has a price tag. Now you have to make a decision: how much are you willing to pay for what you want? Are you willing to pay a lot for the finest chocolate in the store (a Godiva bar)? Or do you want to pay a little less and settle for the chocolate that's maybe not *quite* as good but good nonetheless (a Cadbury bar)? Or maybe you don't want to spend much of anything, so you're willing to settle for a basic kind of chocolate (a Hershey's bar). And as you're leaving the store with your Hershey's bar clutched in your hand, you think, *Hey, who's counting? At least I got chocolate.*

The decision is completely up to you. The minute you enter that store and scan the shelves, *you* decide what you're willing to pay and what you will get in return. The minute you realize it's time to move beyond your adversity, you focus on that spot on the horizon—the one away from the shore—and you decide how much it's worth to reach that spot.

Life is like a game. When you're sidelined by adversity, your job is to do whatever is necessary to get back in the game. If you wait, if you fail to act, if you just pause in the hope that something better will eventually come along, you're saying you no longer want a place in the game. You're even taking a risk that the game may end before you get back in. When you decide that *you're* going to be the one to make the winning shot, you leap off that sideline and grab the ball.

Look at it this way: every single second in life represents the chance for a new beginning. Every single second is an opportunity for you to intentionally choose the direction of your thoughts, words, actions, and path. Best of all, every single second is a new possibility for you to let go of the thing causing you distress— to begin to pull out of the adversity that has been holding you back. Here's what that means: every day consists of 86,400 seconds—86,400 chances to decide to move. To make a fresh start. To forge a new reality. To redefine your future.

By now you know I love to examine the lives of real people who set an incredible example for the rest of us—and I'd now like to share examples of real people who have overcome adversity by changing their reality. I'd like to remind you of a few we've already talked about, but this time I hope to show the changes that led to their ability to overcome adversity. Then I'd like to introduce you to a handful of others who demonstrated great courage and innovation in making the changes needed to set their lives on a new course.

As you'll recall, Albert Einstein didn't talk until he was four, and his school teachers dismissed him as an idiot who would never amount to anything. He did eventually graduate but wasn't able to find a job for two years. When he finally did find employment as an assistant patent examiner, he was passed over for promotion until he "fully mastered machine technology." That was it—he couldn't have cared less about machine technology. Einstein changed his area of emphasis, immersed himself in the study of something he *did* care about, and went on to develop the theory of relativity. This was no idiot; in fact, Einstein is now hailed as one of the great geniuses of the world.

When she was just thirteen, Bethany Hamilton lost her arm in a near-fatal shark attack; knowing she had to change the way she surfed if she still wanted to participate in the sport, she was back on her surfboard a month later, trying out new techniques in an effort to make those changes work. They did: within two years she won first place in the women's division at a national surfing championship.

Bill Gates, now the richest person in the world, couldn't seem to do anything right. When his first business failed, he went back to the drawing board, changed his focus, refined his approach, and came up with Microsoft's first product. The rest is history.

Growing up in a rough Brooklyn neighborhood, Jay-Z always dreamed of making it big as a rapper—but if you remember, not one record label thought he had any talent. Refusing to give up on his dream, he changed direction, creating his own record label and producing his own album. His net worth is now more than $500 million, and *Time* ranked him as one of their Most Influential People in the World in 2013.

As pointed out earlier, Oprah Winfrey was fired from her television job because she "wasn't suited for TV"; analyzing the reason for her failure, she changed her approach, got a new cohost, focused on her love of human-interest stories, and started over again. Those changes led to her multi-award-winning, nationally syndicated talk show, *The Oprah Winfrey Show*, the highest-rated program of its kind in history. She is the greatest black philanthropist in American history and was for a time the world's only black billionaire. And, according to some, she is the most influential woman in the world.

Remember Thomas Edison? Though estimates vary, he apparently suffered anywhere from a thousand to ten thousand failures on his way to inventing the light bulb. Each time, he made subtle changes and tried again. As he told one reporter, he didn't consider his efforts a failure; he "just found ten thousand ways that won't work." But he kept changing what he was doing, and today we have light.

Steven Spielberg, one of the most prolific filmmakers of all time, was refused admission to USC film school—not just once but twice. Instead of letting that obstacle define his future, he changed his approach: he went to California State University at Long Beach and landed a small unpaid-intern job in the editing department at Universal Studios. He figured there was more than one way to learn filmmaking. Want to hear a bit of poetic justice? In the end, USC awarded him an honorary degree in 1994; two years later, he became a trustee of the university.

Spielberg and King barely scratch the surface when it comes to the well-known Hollywood greats who found themselves mired in adversity that could have defeated them and derailed any hope of a career—and who then had to make the changes that would put them back on track. When only child Charlize Theron was fifteen, she watched her mother shoot and kill her alcoholic father in self-defense; Charlize herself endured years of his abuse. That kind of adversity could absolutely paralyze many, but Charlize decided to change the life she had been living so she could make a name for herself. After "not fitting in" where she was attending school, she enrolled in a boarding school, the National School of the Arts in Johannesburg.

A year after her father was killed, Charlize signed a contract as a model and, after working throughout Europe, attended the

Joffrey Ballet School. Having starred in numerous films, she is winner of the Academy Award, Silver Bear, Golden Globe Award, and Screen Actors Guild Award for Best Actress. She is the first South African to win an Academy Award in a major acting category.

Actor Johnny Depp faced intense adversity growing up: his family moved more than twenty times before settling in Miramar, Florida, when he was seven, where they lived in a hotel until his father found work. Depp's adolescence was chaotic: his parents divorced when he was fifteen. Disposed to cutting himself, he started smoking at twelve, lost his virginity at thirteen, started doing drugs at fourteen, and eventually dropped out of high school at sixteen to become a rock musician.

Two weeks later, Depp changed his mind and tried to go back to school. But the principal told him to follow his dream of being a musician. With a determination to change the way he had done things for the first half of his life, he focused on making a success of himself. He began playing with a moderately lucrative band that eventually went to Los Angeles in search of a record deal. While they were unsuccessful, Depp joined another band that was picked up by a label. Within a few years, he was introduced to actor Nicolas Cage, who advised him to pursue a film career.

That advice turned out to be spot-on. Depp's feature films have grossed more than $3.1 billion in the United States and more than $7.6 billion worldwide. He has been nominated numerous times for top awards, winning best actor at the Golden Globes. In 2012, he was listed in the *Guinness Book of World Records* as the highest paid actor, at $75 million. And he has twice been named "Sexiest Man Alive" by *People* magazine.

Actor Tom Cruise grew up in Canada in poverty and dominated by his abusive father—a recipe for certain adversity. Cruise described his father as a bully and coward and "a merchant of chaos" who kept everything in upheaval. "He was the kind of person where, if something goes wrong, they kick you. It was a great lesson in my life—how he'd lull you in, make you feel safe, and then, bang! For me, it was like, 'There's something wrong with this guy. Don't trust him. Be careful around him.'"

Cruise struggled with dyslexia throughout his school years, making things that came easy to everyone else seem almost insurmountable. When he was in the sixth grade, his mother left his father and took Cruise and his sisters to the United States. During high school, he aspired to be a Catholic priest and briefly attended a Franciscan seminary in Cincinnati. During his senior year, he was linebacker on the varsity football team but got cut after he was caught drinking beer before a game. In total, he attended fifteen schools in fourteen years, which obviously created its own kind of chaos.

Determined to change the course of his life, Cruise recaptured a love of acting he had first discovered in the fourth grade, and he vowed to do whatever it took to become a success. Today he is one of Hollywood's highest paid actors; fourteen of his films grossed more than $100 million in the United States, and twenty have grossed more than $200 million worldwide. He has been nominated for three Academy Awards and has won three Golden Globe Awards.

Reality television judge, producer, entrepreneur, and philanthropist Simon Cowell may seem to be an unbridled success, but
before he turned thirty, he had made a million dollars and also *lost*
a million dollars. According to an interview with *The Daily Mail*
in 2012, he suffered through "many failures . . . but [his] record
company going bust, that was the first big one."

It was a monumental loss, but Cowell picked himself up and
determined to change not only the way he was doing things but
the things he was doing. He saw an incredible opportunity in reality television and eventually became the highly rated judge of *Pop
Idol, the X Factor, Britain's Got Talent*, and *American Idol*.

With a current net worth estimated by *Forbes* to be $95 million,
Cowell also changed his focus to one of philanthropy and charity
work. He is a leading patron of Together for Short Lives, the principal U.K. charity for children with life-threatening and life-limiting
conditions. In 2003, he appeared on a charity telethon in Britain
for which viewers pledged thousands to see him get sawn in half.
He is also a prominent supporter of animal rights and produced a
charity single to aid victims of the 2010 earthquake in Haiti.

Examples of the vision and courage to make change aren't, of
course, limited to Hollywood and can be found throughout history. One of the most inspiring is previously mentioned Frederick
Douglass, leader of the abolitionist movement. Born into slavery,
he was separated from his parents and endured horrific violence
before deciding to take charge of his destiny and make the changes
that would expand his possibilities. Teaching himself to read, he

became a living testament against arguments that slaves did not have the intellectual capacity to function as independent American citizens. His insightful and penetrating writing eventually turned the nation's sentiments against slavery, and the once-illiterate, abused boy became a man famous for his dazzling oratory.

Some of the most inspiring examples of transformation are seen in the lives of everyday people. In 2003, Kris Carr was an ordinary thirty-two-year-old New Yorker doing average, routine things and enjoying her life. Then a regular medical checkup resulted in the diagnosis of a rare and incurable stage IV cancer of the lungs and liver.

Doctors gave her no hope of survival, but Carr rose out of that adversity to challenge her diagnosis, harnessing a determination to change her life to one of survival. She attacked her cancer with a revolutionary nutritional lifestyle, incorporated other wellness activities, and, three years after her diagnosis, got married. She then turned her expertise into a series of documentaries, self-help books, and a wellness website that is followed by more than forty thousand people. Winner of a Shorty Award for Best in Healthy Living, she's also won awards for her documentaries *Crazy Sexy Cancer* and *Five Years*. She is now celebrating fifteen years of thriving with cancer, is a *New York Times* and Amazon best-selling author, and is considered one of the most prominent experts on healthy living.

One of the most astonishing examples of change in response to adversity is French actor and author Jean-Dominique Bauby. Former editor-in-chief of *ELLE* magazine, at age forty-three Bauby suffered a massive stroke that affected his brain stem. When he woke up from his coma twenty days later, his mouth, arms, and legs were completely paralyzed; he was entirely speechless and could communicate only by blinking one eye. In the first five months after his stroke, he lost sixty pounds.

Clearly, this was adversity on a monumental scale. And just as clearly, Bauby's career at *ELLE* was over. He had to change, and change quickly. Taking the bull by the horns, he decided to write a memoir detailing his medical ordeal and bearing witness to his determination to live. That's where possibly the most miraculous change had to occur: he could do nothing but blink an eye. It was enough for Bauby. He blinked to select each letter as the alphabet was slowly recited to him, thereby dictating his book one letter at a time.

His memoir, *The Diving Bell and the Butterfly: A Memoir of Life in Death*, was published in France on March 7, 1997. Two days later, Bauby tragically died of pneumonia. His book became a number-one best seller and was adapted into a movie that won numerous awards.

I hope these people have inspired you. I hope, too, that you are ready to move forward in changing your own life circumstances. Before we look at ways you can do that, I want to talk about one more thing that can derail your efforts to change: labeling.

I'm sure you're familiar with labeling, but you may not recognize when it happens, especially if you are labeling yourself. In the way we're using it here, *labeling* means to assign someone to a category or class, especially in a way that is inaccurate or that restricts that person. The problem with labeling of this kind is that it may *sound* all nice and innocent, but by its very nature it squeezes someone into a category that may not make much sense at all. And by its very nature it can make it very difficult for someone to make the changes that are sorely needed.

Why on earth do we label people (including ourselves) anyway? Face it: nothing about life is simple. In fact, much of life is incredibly complicated. In an effort to resolve the complexity of the things around us, we use labeling as a tool to help us sort things and people out. It could be seen as our stab at trying to make sense of all the intricate things that make up our environment. Sadly, negative labeling also contributes to some of our deepest problems and some of the most profound troubles we cause others.

We tend to label people—including ourselves—based on the characteristics they demonstrate all the time. You've probably been guilty of it, because most of us have. Think of the people in your office or your neighborhood or your classroom; I'm betting you've labeled the athlete, the nerd, the musician, the bully. Here's the scary thing: even if your label is an accurate reflection of who that person is right now, it can't possibly reflect who that person will become in the future. Because nobody but God knows what a person will become. Here's an even more important thing to think about: you're labeling someone based on behavior when that behavior may or may not be an accurate reflection of who that person really *is*. Because only God knows the heart.

I think you'll understand exactly what I'm saying when you consider the label *bully*. Let's say you label someone a bully. You mean that he tends to bully other people. But it doesn't stop there. Your label is *also* saying something about who that person is at his core: the kind of person who bullies others. You are saying something central about that person. And if that person adopts that label and really believes it of himself, he's soon stuck with it. If he does bully someone, he now has further evidence that he is a bad person instead of a good person who made a bad decision. And when the label gets really firmly attached, suddenly he believes, "That's just who I am, and I can't change."

Consider the damage that label caused.

Sadly, we are too often too quick to label, and the consequences can be devastating. One classic study[27] done decades ago is still the standard in demonstrating the danger of labeling. In the study, a group of college students watched a video of a fourth grader named Hannah playing in what they believed to be her neighborhood; they also read a fact sheet about Hannah that allegedly described her background.

Half the students watched Hannah playing in what was obviously an affluent, tree-lined, middle-class neighborhood. The fact sheet described her parents as college-educated professionals. The other half of the students watched a video of Hannah playing in what appeared to be a low-income housing project. The fact sheet these students read described Hannah's parents as high-school graduates with blue-collar jobs.

---

27 See J. M. Darley and P. H. Gross, "A Hypothesis-Confirming Bias in Labeling Effects," *Journal of Personality and Social Psychology*, 44, 20–33.

The students were then asked to assess Hannah's academic ability by watching a video of her responding to a series of achievement test questions. Hannah performed brilliantly: she answered some of the tough questions easily and correctly but sometimes answered some of the easier questions incorrectly, and then only after struggling to come up with her response. In reality, it was difficult to discern exactly what kind of academic ability Hannah had.

The students who watched the videos didn't have a problem labeling Hannah, though—and they did it based on her socioeconomic status, *not* her actual academic performance. The ones who labeled Hannah as "middle-class" rated her as performing close to a fifth-grade level. The students who labeled Hannah as "poor" rated her as performing below a fourth-grade level.

I've been labeled a lot in my life, fortunately in positive ways. When I was a little girl, my older family members and friends labeled me as "fast." My most recent (or should I say my last) ex-husband labeled me when he said, "I know you will make it." My best friend gave me a similar label when she said, "You will be fine no matter what you're dealing with; there's no need to worry about you." Some of my friends labeled me as "lucky." Some of my Christian brothers and sisters labeled me as "blessed."

What did those labels say about me? Without me even realizing it, those labels shaped and defined who I was—and, even more profoundly, who I would become—because they *propelled* me to do my very best and to be the very best I could be.

Now let's look at how I labeled myself as a result: "driven and destined for success." I knew in my heart that nothing was unmanageable and unattainable, and I decided very consciously that I would act on that belief. I remember seeing a quote by the legendary actress Audrey Hepburn that really resonated with me: "Nothing is impossible; the word itself says 'I'm possible.'"

So that's what I adopted for myself. I decided what I wanted, went after it, and with God's grace and mercy, He always provided. Don't think for a minute I didn't have issues and problems; just like everyone else, I had my fair share. But I always managed to move beyond obstacles and reach the finish line.

Then came the big one: I was enjoying the fruits of my labors. I had been recognized and awarded for my work. And just when I thought I was flying high, along came that CFO. You remember, the one who was keeping two sets of books. The rest is history. Ultimately, I lost my business, my home, my marriage, and my mojo. Suddenly my carefully applied label was in shreds and my life no longer made any sense. I had been mislabeled, or so I thought.

Luckily for me, I did *not* lose my belief in myself and my ability to rise above whatever life threw in my path even though my label had been torn away. Fortunately, those labels weren't the kind that hurt me or held me back. I did lose a lot of things, but I renewed and deepened my relationship with God. And with His guidance and direction, I embarked on a whole new journey that has been one of the most satisfying of my life.

The primary danger with negative labeling is that it precludes change. It convinces us that we are somehow permanently assigned to a particular category or class. It also convinces us that such will never change—that *we* can never change. The amount of harm that results from that invalid thinking is difficult to describe.

Another danger is that labeling can permanently relegate someone to a "lower" category, class, group, or type—one from which that person may never escape if the label is compelling enough.

Think of how dangerous this kind of labeling could be if done by a teacher! Well, we have convincing evidence of exactly *how* dangerous based on the results of another fascinating study.[28] And this one's a killer.

The researchers told teachers at an elementary school that some of their students had scored in the top 20 percent of a test designed to identify what they called "academic bloomers"—students who were expected to experience intense intellectual development during the next year. But that wasn't true. In fact, the students in the so-called "bloomers" group were actually chosen at random from all the kids in the school—and they had done no better than their classmates on the academic test. But nobody told the teachers that. The teachers were convinced they had a handful of geniuses on their hands, and they were off to the races.

What happened next was absolutely frightening in terms of impact. A year later, the researchers returned to the school and

---

28 See Robert Rosenthal and Lenore Jacobson, *Pygmalion in the Classroom*, expanded edition (New York: Irvington, 1992).

administered the same test to all the students. They called the test results "astonishing"—the children who had been labeled as "bloomers" now scored fully fifteen IQ points higher than their classmates who had not been classified in their group. The difference had nothing to do with the students. It had *everything* to do with the teachers, who labeled them as academically gifted and who fostered their intellectual development, creating a self-fulfilling prophecy in which the students who were *expected* to bloom significantly outperformed their classmates—even though the expectation was unjustified.

What about the kids who weren't labeled as "bloomers"? They were left in the dust. They too performed as expected: they were average. Nobody shined or improved by leaps and bounds, even though they had every bit the academic potential of those labeled as "bloomers."

Labeling can be particularly damaging when it comes to race. A group of white students at Stanford was shown a picture of a man who was racially indistinct—he could have been labeled as "black," but he could have just as convincingly been labeled as "white."[29] Half the students were told the man was white. The other half were told the man was black. The students were then given four minutes to draw the face as they saw it on the screen in front of them.

Get ready for some more astonishing results. Even though *all the students were looking at the same face*, the ones who thought they

---

29 See J. L. Eberhardt, N. Dasgupta, and T. L. Banaszynski, "Believing Is Seeing: The Effects of Racial Labels and Implicit Beliefs on Face Perception," *Personality and Social Psychology Bulletin*, 29 (2003), 360–70.

were looking at a black man drew facial features stereotypical of the black race. In other words, their racial labels became a powerful lens through which the students "saw" that man—and they were incapable of seeing him independently of that label.

Now can you see why labeling is so dangerous? Is it possible the people we label as rich, poor, black, white, smart, or stupid may actually become richer, poorer, blacker, whiter, smarter, or stupider just because they are labeled that way? Is it possible you could get stuck in adversity and be unable to make the necessary changes because *you've* been labeled a certain way? Tennis great Martina Navratilova put it perfectly when she said, "Labels are for filing. Labels are for clothing. Labels are not for people."

Remember that you can do incredible harm labeling others, but you can also do inconceivable harm when you label yourself. Behavioral scientist and author Steve Maraboli pointed out, "I used to worry about the labels others place on me, until I realized my limitations weren't coming from their labels, but from my own."

As you determine to reinvent your adversity and make the changes you need in your life, avoid the trap of labeling yourself. As American country legend Jimmy Dean said, "I can't change the direction of the wind, but I can adjust my sails to always reach my destination." Don't create an unnecessarily stiff wind in your life by slapping labels on yourself. And never lose belief that you *can* adjust your sails, no matter what kind of wind is howling. Even if the wind rips through your life at hurricane velocity, remember the sage words of business magnate Henry Ford, who faced more than his share of adversity: "When everything seems to be going against you, remember that the airplane takes off against the wind, not with it."

What, then, can you do to change? First of all, you need to decide—*really* decide—that it's worth it to make a change. After all, life is tough, and the path of least resistance sometimes consists of just giving up. And sometimes things just seem to get harder and harder, so it can be overwhelming to even consider change. You're the only one who can decide something different for yourself. And that's the first step.

With that, you also need to believe in yourself. If you don't believe, it's likely you'll be forever stuck in your circumstances, as difficult as they are. When you don't believe, you will continue to suffer doubt, depression, negativity, and distress. Instead of envisioning change, you'll probably say to yourself, "Oh, well. That's just life." But that's *not* just life. Life isn't supposed to be something you just endure—it's supposed to be filled with adventure and things to look forward to. I have always loved the advice of U.S. president Theodore Roosevelt: "Believe you can, and you're halfway there."

When you simply believe, you discover the opposite is true: anything is possible. And when anything is possible, there are endless ways to change your circumstances. You'll start to gravitate toward people who encourage and inspire you. Start with some of the stories in this book; add to that by actively looking for inspiring stories, quotes, and scriptures. If you can, start each day reading or watching something that inspires you. You'll see ways of approaching things differently that will enable you to make changes that will improve things, often in dramatic ways. Best of all, your focus will no longer be on the adversity but on what you can do about it.

As you work to reinvent adversity and make positive changes, one of the best things you can do is really define your passion in life—the thing that makes you light up inside and that gives you a reason to get up in the morning. We talked about Tom Cruise: after finding himself going around in aimless circles after years of adversity, he started thinking about what gave him purpose—and he rediscovered his love of acting, something he hadn't thought about since elementary school. Determined to find joy in something again, he threw himself into acting and ended up changing his life.

Once you find and follow your passion, you will see that you are happier, that you smile more, that you're more positive, and that you are more creative. All this can have the significant result of helping pull you away from the adversity that's been holding you back.

Pursuing your passion will probably require that you get out of your usual routine, try something different, or develop a new habit. Any and all of these are great ways to start reinventing your adversity. Along with getting your creative juices flowing, you'll get to experience new things and may just find something completely different that changes everything.

Be aware that making change takes hard work: *you're* the one who needs to put in the effort and invest the blood, sweat, and tears to make it happen. Nobody else can do it for you. That may sound like too much right now—and you may worry that all the things happening in your life are already sucking up every sliver of strength and energy you have. You may honestly believe you don't have anything left in reserve, nothing to invest in any kind of brand-new endeavor. Believe me: just *try*. I'm convinced you will surprise even yourself with what you can pull out of the depths of that beat-up soul. I know—and deep down inside, you know—that you are much stronger than you think. So dig deep down, tap into your inner strength, and make it happen.

The very best changes, the ones that will bring the greatest rewards, take the most work to accomplish. One of the keys to doing that work is to connect with others, especially people who inspire you, share your passion, have similar interests, and can support you in your efforts. Adversity tends to isolate you—you find yourself withdrawing in an attempt to just make it through. But staying connected to other people is key to everything in life—including your health! Numerous studies by respected researchers show that the social support that comes from being connected protects us against the damaging effects of stress,[30] including the disruption that often accompanies adversity; improves heart health;[31] boosts immunity;[32] and may even help you live longer.[33]

---

30 S. Cohen, B. H. Gottlieb, and L. G. Underwood, "Social Relationships and Health," in S. Cohen, L. G. Underwood, and B. H. Gottlieb, eds., *Measuring and Intervening in Social Support* (New York: Oxford University Press, 2000), 3–25.

31 "Enriching Mental Health Good for the Heart," *Harvard Health Letter* 14, no. 1 (September 1, 2003).

32 S. Kennedy, J. Kiecolt-Glaser, and R. Glaser, "Immunological Consequences of Acute and Chronic Stressors: Mediating Role of Interpersonal Relationships," *British Journal of Medical Psychology* 61:77–85.

33 Julianne Holt-Lunstead, Timothy B. Smith, and J. Bradley Layton, "Social Relationships and Mortality Risk: A Meta-Analytic Review," *PLoS Medicine* 7, no. 7 (2010).

Once you start down the path to change, do whatever you can to keep your desire strong. That desire will determine whether you follow through and make the change or whether you sink back into the adversity and simply give up. In order to keep your desire strong, you'll have to do the things I've already talked about in this book: Muster the courage to keep going. Be willing to get back up, dust yourself off, and move forward again every time you fall down. Refuse to let failure define you. Sharpen your vision. Surround yourself with those who will support and encourage you.

And whatever you do, do it *now*. Stop waiting. Change is not going to occur on its own, no matter how long you wait or how fervently you wish for it unless *you* take the steps to make it happen. In the words of Mark Twain, "Twenty years from now you will be more disappointed by the things that you didn't do than by the ones you did do, so throw off the bowlines, sail away from safe harbor, catch the trade winds in your sails. Explore. Dream. Discover."

Chapter Six

Joy in the Journey

Focus on the journey, not the destination.
Joy is found not in finishing an activity
but in doing it.

—*Greg Anderson*

H elen Keller referred to joy as "an invincible host against difficulties." That's a critically important thing to remember as you endure adversity. So are the sage words of American author and anthropologist Carlos Castaneda: "We either make ourselves happy or miserable. The amount of work is the same."

By now you know all about adversity. So do I. You and I both know that it can sap your energy and cause the smallest "extra" demand to seem more like a Mount Everest than anything else. So Castaneda begs an interesting question: If it takes as much work to feel miserable as it does to feel happy, who wouldn't want to choose happiness?

There is something almost blissful to consider about adversity. In a very real way, it paves the path to joy. Try to envision the scene created by poet Jalaluddin Rumi: "Sorrow prepares you for joy. It violently sweeps everything out of your house, so that new joy can find space to enter. It shakes the yellow leaves from the bough of your heart, so that fresh, green leaves can grow in their place. It pulls up the rotten roots, so that new roots hidden beneath have room to grow. Whatever sorrow shakes from your heart, far better things will take their place." What a concept—the adversity through which you are now struggling is, in a very real way, preparing your soul for the advent of joy.

Believe it or not, there's another crucial connection between adversity and joy. American musician Carlos Santana pointed out that "if you carry joy in your heart, you can heal any moment." Those include every single moment of adversity. And that's the miracle for which you are wishing and working: the healing that will enable you to transform your life from one of agony to one of achievement—and, yes, to one of joy.

What, then, is joy? The dictionary defines it as a feeling of great pleasure and happiness, a state of happiness or felicity, or a source or cause of delight. The dictionary also provides a substantial list of synonyms for *joy*, among them *jubilation, bliss, triumph, exultation, gladness, glee, exhilaration, euphoria, ecstasy,* and *rapture.* I personally favor the definition of French philosopher and Jesuit priest Pierre Teilhard de Chardin, a trained paleontologist who participated in the discovery of Peking Man. He wrote, "Joy is the infallible sign of the presence of God."

At any rate, you get the drift. But here's something important to remember about joy: while the word *happiness* is often used to define or describe joy, the two are *not* the same. There are some fundamental differences between joy and happiness, and understanding those differences is an important step toward attaining the joy that will help you heal from adversity.

If I had to sum it up succinctly, I'd explain that *happiness* is an emotion caused by an external event; rather than being caused by a particular event, *joy* is a deep sense of contentment that comes from within. I want to make sure you understand the essential differences between joy and happiness because, while it seems counterintuitive, confusion between the two can actually result in unhappiness—or even misery. Why? When you set out in search of happiness, all kinds of things can go wrong. When you seek joy, on the other hand, you make changes to *yourself* instead of your *circumstances*, and those changes help you find lasting joy.

Here's how it works. *Happiness*, as I already mentioned, is external. It's based on people, places, things, events, or situations—many of which you can't control. You're counting on those outside people, places, things, events, or situations to line up with your expectations of them, which you are convinced will make you happy. *Joy*, on the other hand, is internal. It comes from when you make peace with who you are, where you are, and why you are—not on the who, where, or why of anyone else.

Happiness is also extremely subjective. Generally speaking, you're happy if you *perceive* you're happy. Happiness can actually be scientifically studied for that very reason—it's relatively easy for a person to report their level of happiness on a scale. Not so with joy. Joy is a state of mind, something localized in the heart. It encompasses things like confidence, contentment, and hope.

Often, happiness is off somewhere in the future. You'll be happy when you're able to buy a house. You'll be happy when you lose all that weight. You'll be happy when you meet the right person. You'll be happy when you get out of debt. You'll be happy when your alcoholic spouse finally agrees to counseling. Happiness is not only oriented to the future, it requires that you put all your eggs in someone else's basket—and that's a dangerous place for your eggs to be. Joy, instead, isn't dependent on anyone else; in fact, it's not contingent on anything.

Because happiness depends on external factors, it is usually transitory—short-lived, temporary, ephemeral, whatever term you want to attach to it. Going shopping with a good friend may make you feel happy, but sooner or later the shopping trip ends, the friend goes home, and so do you. Landing a job as a model may make you happy, but you will inevitably get too old or develop too many wrinkles to keep your job. Getting a new car may make you happy, but that happiness vanishes when your car is totaled in a head-on collision. Buying your dream house may make you happy, but when your CFO keeps two sets of books and you lose your business, you may also lose your dream house. Ask me. I know. Happiness is like the bubbles in a glass of champagne—delightful but inevitably fleeting. Joy is like oxygen; it's always there. Joy can last forever. It's part of what's inside, and it won't go away because the shopping trip ends, the career is over, the car is wrecked, or the dream house goes back on the market. Abiding joy is a stillness and a peace that exists between you and God, and it's not shaken by anything.

Here's the most amazing aspect of the difference between happiness and joy: you can feel great joy even while you're dealing with some pretty ragged unhappiness. English crime novelist Agatha Christie captured that feeling when she wrote, "I like living. I have sometimes been wildly, despairingly, acutely miserable, wracked with sorrow, but through it all I still know quite certainly that just to be alive is a grand thing."

Because joy is the stuff of your essence, the fiber of your soul, once you discover joy, it is always there, no matter what other emotions may slide in. Here's what that means: It's possible to grieve with your whole heart but still have joy. It's possible to be so wrecked and battered you feel like you have been pulled through a knothole backward but still have joy. It's possible to get dumped, dumped on, rejected, abandoned, betrayed, fired, and still have joy. It's possible to be going through what *has* to be the worst thing that's ever happened and still feel joy.

One psychologist explained it this way: "You don't have to have 'him' for the holidays to have joy. Likewise, you don't have to get revenge, snoop out his shortcomings, tell the new girlfriend the truth, or anything else in order to have joy. You can lose in court with him, already have lost your life savings to him, watch him out with a new woman, or live out of the back of your car and still have joy."[34]

The same psychologist looked to her own mother for a staggering example of the difference between happiness and joy: Her mother's "pathological man ran off with her life savings forcing her to work well past retirement. It forced her to live simply, so she moved to a one-room beach shack and drove a motorcycle. For cheap entertainment, she walked the beach and painted nudes. She drank cheap grocery store wine that came in a box, bought her clothes from thrift shops, and made beach totes from crocheting plastic grocery bags together. She recycled long before it was hip to do it. But what she recycled most and best was pain . . . into joy. . . . It was both an enigma and a privilege to watch this magnificent life emerge from the ashes of great betrayal."[35]

Canadian author and inspirational speaker Danielle Laporte summed it up beautifully when she wrote, "It has never failed that when I have been through the most heart-breaking passages of my life—betrayal, financial hardship, divorce, dreams dashed—the pain brought me to the floor of my being, and what was there to be found? The simple joy of being alive."[36]

As you begin to reinvent your adversity, here's the most important thing you can remember: true joy is in the *journey*, not the destination. If you think joy will occur only when the adversity ends—only

---

34 Sandra L. Brown, "Joy-VS-Happiness," *Psychology Today*, December 18, 2012.
35 Ibid.
36 (http://www.daniellelaporte.com/definition-of-happiness-and-why-its-different-from-joy/)

when you finally resolve the money problems or the health issues or the relationship complications—you will rob yourself of the incredible joy you can be feeling right now. You will never fully find joy because it will always be around the next bend in the road.

I've talked about life as a magnificent trip. Imagine you're going on a trip and you think, *As soon as I get there, I'll have complete joy.* Imagine you just grit your teeth while you're on your way to wherever you're going because you're not expecting any joy until you get there. Now imagine you reach your destination and things aren't anything like you imagined. The accommodations are horrible— your hotel room is dank and the bed is lumpy. The weather is a nightmare; freezing rain and howling winds are whipping through the area. Your luggage is lost, and you have nothing but the clothes on your back. And the people who were supposed to be there to meet you failed to show up. Look at all the time you wasted on the journey to your destination—precious time when you could have been appreciating the view from the airplane window, the delightful person in the seat next to you, even the crunchy peanuts the flight attendant handed out.

Never waste the opportunity to experience joy to its fullest. Never put joy on hold. Never decide that joy will be better, richer, deeper, more complete somewhere *else*. Because when you make that decision, you'll never arrive somewhere *else*. Instead, embrace joy wherever you are, even if you are in the middle of an angry storm of adversity. Because it's still possible to feel remarkable joy even in that situation, and joy is what will allow you to move forward.

When we talk about someone who learned to feel joy in the midst of an unbelievable storm of adversity, we have to revisit the life of Nelson Mandela. At the beginning of his life sentence and incarceration at Robben Island, South Africa's version of Alcatraz, the warder's first words to Mandela when he arrived were "This is the Island. This is where you will die."[37]

Few of us can even imagine the scope of Mandela's adversity during his incarceration. He was prisoner 46664—the 466th prisoner to arrive in 1964—and was confined to a seven-foot-square concrete cell in a new cell block specifically constructed to house political prisoners. He slept on the floor and had only a slop bucket for a toilet. During the day, he was sentenced to hard labor in a limestone quarry, where he crushed stones with a hammer to make gravel; the blindingly bright sun did permanent damage to his eyes. The damp conditions on the island and in the prison likely contributed to the tuberculosis he contracted.

Just two years after being sent to Robben Island, Mandela drew his line in the sand in a statement before the South African Supreme Court: "I have cherished the ideal of a democratic and free society in which all persons will live together in harmony and with equal opportunities. It is an ideal which I hope to live for. But, my lord, if needs be, it is an ideal for which I am prepared to die."

At first, Mandela was not allowed any reading materials. He was allowed only one visitor a year, and that visit could last only thirty

---

37 Mike Wooldridge, "Mandela Death: How He Survived 27 Years in Prison," BBC News, December 11, 2013.

minutes. And that's not all: he could write and receive only one letter every six months.

On the occasions when he complained to prison officials over his ill treatment, he was punished by being locked up in solitary confinement. "In those early years, isolation became a habit," he wrote in his autobiography, *The Long Walk to Freedom*. "We were routinely charged for the smallest infractions and sentenced to isolation. . . . I found solitary confinement the most forbidding aspect of prison life. There was no end and no beginning; there is only one's own mind, which can begin to play tricks."

Even when he wasn't in solitary confinement, he had little opportunity to communicate with others, at least for much of his incarceration. At 4:00 p.m., he was locked in a cell and prohibited from even talking to the other inmates within hearing range. Once the cell doors were closed at four, the prisoners were not allowed to speak.

Mandela managed to challenge and change that situation, however. In an interview with Oprah Winfrey following his release from prison, he said, "The officers who were senior to the wardens treated them like vermin, but because we treated the wardens with respect, they helped us. Once the cells were locked and the senior officers went away, the wardens allowed us to do anything except open the cell doors, because they didn't have keys. They let us speak to those in the cells opposite us. As a result of the way we treated the wardens, they tended to become good people."

Mandela did other things to show respect to those who oppressed him. When he arrived in prison, he was a trained lawyer. He found that when the wardens received letters of summons or demands, they didn't have the resources to seek help from an attorney. Mandela generously helped them settle their cases without any charge to them. As a result, many became attached to him.

In his interview with Oprah Winfrey, she asked if he believed people were good at their core. "There is no doubt whatsoever," he answered her. "Those of us in the fight against apartheid changed many people who hated us because they discovered that we respected them." And when she asked how he could respect people who oppressed him, he answered, "You must understand that people get caught up in the policy of their country. In prison, for instance, a warden or officer is not promoted if he doesn't follow the policy of the government—though he himself does not believe in that policy."

Mandela's ability to soften the wardens is similar to another way his time in prison affected him. In a brief interview with Mandela, a reporter from CNN asked how Mandela was able to emerge from prison without hating white people. Mandela's answer "surprised" the reporter: "If I had allowed myself to become bitter, I would have died in prison," Mandela explained. The reporter observed that "what prison helped Mandela understand was that even a black president who had been denied full citizenship in his country could not let hate—even the anger that hate begot—have the last word."[38]

During his eighteen years at Robben Island, Mandela became possibly the world's most famous political prisoner but also the world's least recognizable one. During those years, the only people who saw him were his jailers, his fellow inmates, and a handful of family members. South Africa's white government leaders, in an attempt to diminish his reputation, refused to release any photos of Mandela during the years he was in prison.

Mandela himself was very fond of telling a story about how, after fifteen years at Robben Island, he was taken five miles to the mainland and into Cape Town for a medical checkup. During that trip, his prison warders generously granted his request that he be allowed to stroll on the beach for just a few minutes. According to the story, "Walking on the beach, Mandela, the world's most famous political prisoner, was anonymous. Having been in jail since the early 1960s, and his pictures banned from being circulated in public or published in the media, very few people knew his appearance. On the beach that day, no one as much as glanced at him. Later, with a glint in his eye, Mandela said he'd wondered what would have happened had he suddenly shouted: 'I am Nelson Mandela.'"[39]

After eighteen brutal years at Robben Island, Mandela was moved to Pollsmoor Prison on the South African mainland.

---

38 Sylvester Monroe, "Nelson Mandela's Leadership Born Out of Adversity," CNN, December 10, 2013.
39 "Mandela Death: How a Prisoner Became a Legend," BBC News, December 7, 2013.

Conditions there were slightly improved over what he had endured at Robben. His final years in prison were spent in a cottage he had to himself in the garden of Victor Verster, a jail near Cape Town. While he had television, radio, newspapers, a swimming pool, and any visitors he wanted, he was still in jail.

Of the twenty-seven total years he spent in prison, Robben Island was "the crucible which transformed him. Through his intelligence, charm and dignified defiance, Mandela eventually bent even the most brutal prison officials to his will, assumed leadership over his jailed comrades and became the master of his own prison. He emerged from it the mature leader who would fight and win the great political battles that would create a new democratic South Africa."[40]

In 1994, Mandela returned to Robben Island as a visitor and reflected on his time there when he said, "Wounds that can't be seen are more painful than those that can be seen and cured by a doctor. One of the saddest moments of my life in prison was the death of my mother. The next shattering experience was the death of my eldest son in a car accident." He was denied permission to attend either funeral.[41]

Many in his situation would have lost hope, but not Mandela. In fact, according to him, it was during his life sentence that he discovered life and joy. His attitude toward his years in prison demonstrates his determination to confront adversity with joy: "I went for a long holiday for twenty-seven years."

---

40 "The Long Walk of Nelson Mandela: An Intimate Portrait of One of the 20th Century's Greatest Leaders," *Frontline*.
41 Wooldridge.

"His genius was in his pragmatism—his generosity of spirit," said one reporter for National Public Radio. "What set him apart from his fellow detainees was that he was wise enough to be influenced by new ideas and in turn was able to soften and broaden the minds of other young radicals."[42]

Of his release from prison, Oprah Winfrey said, "This is a moment I will never forget: Nelson Mandela, a man sentenced to life in prison because of his fight to end segregation in South Africa, walking away free after 27 years. As I watched him emerge from a car that day in 1990, I felt what many around the world did—overwhelming hope and joy. That Mandela survived was a testament to the power of the human spirit to overcome *anything*."[43]

Mandela himself echoed that conviction in a letter from prison to his wife, Winnie: "Difficulties break some men but make others. No axe is sharp enough to cut the soul of a sinner who keeps on trying, one armed with the hope that he will rise even in the end."

In his own words, Mandela demonstrated why his sense of joy enabled him to not only survive an ordeal that would have defeated many but to go on to even greater things: "I have walked that long road to freedom. I have tried not to falter; I have made missteps along the way. But I have discovered the secret that after climbing a great hill, one only finds that there are many more hills to climb. I have taken a moment here to rest, to steal a view of the glorious vista

---

42 Greg Myre, "The Day Nelson Mandela Walked Out of Prison," NPR, June 27, 2013.
43 Oprah Winfrey, "Oprah Talks to Nelson Mandela," Oprah.com, from an interview published in *O Magazine*, 2001.

that surrounds me, to look back on the distance I have come. But I can rest only for a moment, for with freedom comes responsibilities, and I dare not linger, for my long walk is not yet ended."

Perhaps his ability to reinvent his adversity was linked to his attitude of joy, for as he explained, "I am fundamentally an optimist. Whether that comes from nature or nurture, I cannot say. Part of being optimistic is keeping one's head pointed toward the sun, one's feet moving forward. There were many dark moments when my faith in humanity was sorely tested, but I would not and could not give myself up to despair. That way lays defeat and death."

When we give in to adversity, we choose defeat and death. When we actively look for joy and allow ourselves to find it whenever it may be—even in the darkest, most abysmal corner of a seven-foot-square concrete cell—it has the power to change our lives.

While Mandela's adversity was severe and his discovery of joy sublime, he is not alone; there are many throughout history—including in our day—who have also embraced joy even during struggle. You may be personally acquainted with some of them. You may even be one of them.

I'd like to share a little bit about another person who suffered tremendous adversity yet exuded a sense of soaring joy that impacted her entire life. Borghild Margrethe Dahl was born in Minnesota in 1890, the daughter of Norwegians who had immigrated to the United States just ten years before she was born. She suffered severely impaired vision from birth and also the disfigurement of having only one eye.

Despite her near blindness, she desperately wanted to participate in all the things everyone else did, refusing to be pitied or considered "different." Through sheer determination, she succeeded in almost everything she tried. As a child, she wanted to play hopscotch with the other children, but her eyesight was so bad she couldn't see the lines on the ground. Dahl didn't let that stop her. After the other children went home, she got down on the ground and crawled along with her eye near the marks. She memorized every bit of the ground where she and her friends played and where the marks were drawn, and soon she became an expert at hopscotch.

Dahl did all her reading at home. In her autobiography, she wrote, "I had only one eye, and it was so covered with dense scars that I had to do all my seeing through one small opening in the left of the eye. I could see a book only by holding it up close to my face and by straining my one eye as hard as I could to the left."[44] She held the large-print book so close to her eye that her eyelashes brushed the pages.

Educators tried to discourage her from pursuing an education since they believed her impaired eyesight would make it impossible for her to do the required work. But they didn't know Dahl and couldn't appreciate the joy she felt in learning. She attended and received a bachelor of arts degree from the University of Minnesota before going on to study at Columbia University and receiving a scholarship to the University of Oslo.

The woman whom educators gave no hope started teaching in the small village of Twin Valley, Minnesota, where she did so until

---

44 Borghild Dahl, *I Wanted to See* (New York: Macmillan, 1944), 1.

she became a professor of journalism, literature, and Norwegian at Augustana College in Sioux Falls, South Dakota, in the 1930s. She taught there for thirteen years, lecturing before women's clubs and giving radio talks about books and authors. She also eventually became the principal of eight schools in western Minnesota and North Dakota. Of those days, Dahl wrote, "In the back of my mind there had always lurked a fear of total blindness. In order to overcome this, I had adopted a cheerful, almost hilarious, attitude toward life."

That fear became reality when in 1939 she did become completely blind. What would have been a hopeless setback for others merely spurred Dahl on to greater challenges she faced with dogged determination.

Then a miracle occurred. In 1943, when Dahl was fifty-three years old, a revolutionary vision-correction procedure was developed and made available at Mayo Clinic. Dahl had the surgery, and it restored much of her vision, enabling her to see forty times as well as she had ever been able to before.

To this woman who had nurtured joy and gratitude throughout her life, a whole new world of even greater joy opened up. With her newfound vision, it was thrilling to Dahl even to wash dishes in the kitchen sink. "I begin to play with the white fluffy suds in the dishpan," she wrote. "I dip my hands into them and I pick up a ball of tiny soap bubbles. I hold them up against the light and in each of them, I can see the brilliant colors of a miniature rainbow."

As she looked through the window above the kitchen sink, she saw "the flapping gray-back wings of the sparrows flying through the thick, falling snow." Her joy in even the simplest things in life was so profound she closed her autobiography, *I Wanted to See*, with these words: "Our Father in heaven, I thank Thee. I thank Thee."[45]

Once her eyesight was restored, Dahl turned her focus to writing. In addition to her autobiography, which was published in 1944 to great critical acclaim, she wrote fifteen other books, most for young people and most based on her experiences growing up as the daughter of Norwegian parents living in the Midwest. In 1950, she received the Medal of St. Olav from King Haakon VII of Norway for her work in international relations. The medal is awarded in recognition of "outstanding services rendered in connection with the spreading of information about Norway abroad and for strengthening the bonds between expatriate Norwegians and their home country."

Dahl's last book, *Happy All My Life*, was published in 1982 when she was ninety-two. It was a title particularly well-suited to a woman who clung to hope and felt deep joy despite her significant challenges. She passed away two years later in 1984 at the age of ninety-four.

Some of the best examples of people who chose joy are in scripture, and I'd like to share a few from the Bible who illustrate the ability to adopt joy regardless of what is going on around them. One of those is Joseph, the son of Jacob and Rachel; he was clearly his father's favorite and was given the coat of many colors to signify his position as heir. That may have been a thrill for Joseph, but it didn't sit well with his brothers; after all, he was the youngest, and

---

45 Dahl, 210.

they felt he had no business being chosen as heir. He also got special privileges: while they were hard at work all day with the sheep, Joseph got to spend his days in leisure at his father's feet.

As is easy to imagine, his brothers began to resent him. That resentment grew into bitterness and hatred. One thing led to another, and the brothers stripped Joseph of his coat, cast him into a pit, and sold him into slavery. But that didn't defeat Joseph. Instead, he maintained his faith and joy in the Lord, knowing that God had a plan for his life even though it was difficult to imagine in the midst of his adversity.

The story actually had a happy ending despite some famine and what had to be some embarrassment on the part of Joseph's brothers when they realized it was he who was second in command to Pharaoh. Why? Because Joseph was focused more on his joy and sense of inner peace than on retribution against his brothers, and all was forgiven. He even determined there was a purpose behind all his adversity, as he was able to save a nation from starvation: "But as for you, ye thought evil against me; but God meant it unto good, to bring to pass, as it is this day, to save much people alive" (Genesis 50:20).

Or consider the example of Ruth. Ruth and her mother-in-law, Naomi, were both in an extremely difficult circumstance: they had both been widowed and, according to the customs of the day, were without men to take care of them, leaving them destitute. Naomi decided to return to Judah, where she had family, and told Ruth to go back to her family, where she could hopefully find someone to marry her and take care of her.

But Ruth didn't want to leave Naomi: Ruth had come to love the God Naomi worshipped and therein found her joy. Rather than go back to her culture, where she would be expected to worship idols, Ruth told her mother-in-law, "Entreat me not to leave thee, or to return from following after thee: for whither thou goest, I will go; and where thou lodgest, I will lodge: thy people shall be my people, and thy God my God" (Ruth 1:16).

Naomi allowed Ruth to come with her back to Judah, and Ruth demonstrated her great joy by doing everything she could to help Naomi—including gathering the leftover heads of grain in the fields for their support. In His great wisdom, God loved and honored both women by blessing Ruth with a husband and child and Naomi with a grandson who became the grandfather of King David.

And what of Jacob, the son of Isaac and Rebekah and twin to Esau? He was running for his life and sought refuge at the house and farm of his uncle, Laban. He was penniless and unemployed until Laban offered him a job. When he tried to negotiate the wages for Jacob's work, Jacob offered to work for free on one condition: "And Jacob loved Rachel; and said, I will serve thee seven years for Rachel thy younger daughter" (Genesis 29:18).

Work for seven years without pay? It was an astonishing offer, but Laban agreed to the terms. Then, we are told, "And Jacob served seven years for Rachel; and they seemed unto him but a few days, for the love he had to her" (Genesis 29:20).

We can only imagine the joy Jacob felt during those seven years knowing that his efforts were leading him ever closer to the woman he loved so deeply. Many others would have resisted such servitude, but this young man harnessed his inner joy to carry him through to the end. We can then more easily imagine what must have been profound disappointment when, after seven long years, Laban changed the terms of the agreement. On their wedding night, it wasn't Rachel at the altar but Leah—Rachel's older sister. After all, said Laban, it wasn't fitting that the younger daughter should marry first.

Most would have been angry over that deception. Many would have simply refused; after all, he had spent *seven long years* toiling for no monetary compensation, all in anticipation of marrying Rachel. Seeing Leah all decked out in her wedding gown must have been a sore disappointment. But Jacob was a man filled with joy regardless of circumstance. So he fulfilled his obligation to Laban by marrying Leah. And then? He worked *another seven years without pay* for the privilege of taking Rachel to wed. He was a man who kept his promises, and God honored him with a large family and great wealth.

One of the greatest examples of joy in the scriptures is the Apostle Paul, who also managed to find joy no matter his circumstances. And his circumstances were, by any standard, pretty grim. He received thirty-nine stripes, was beaten three times with rods, and was stoned. He was shipwrecked. He withstood many perils: perils of waters, of robbers, of the Gentiles, in the city, in the wilderness, in the sea, and of his own countrymen. And he was persecuted—though as he is quick to tell us, "Persecuted, but not forsaken; struck down, but not destroyed" (Philippians 4:9).

Paul was often sleep-deprived, hungry, and thirsty. He fasted often. More often than not, he was cold and naked. And then there was this: "And lest I should be exalted above measure through the abundance of the revelations, there was given to me a thorn in the flesh, the messenger of Satan to buffet me, lest I should be exalted above measure" (2 Corinthians 12:7). That blasted thorn.

I think we can all agree Paul was a case study in adversity. Yet look at some of the things he wrote to the Saints in Philippi, and see what you think about his joy barometer:

- "Therefore, my brethren dearly beloved and longed for, my joy and crown, so stand fast in the Lord, my dearly beloved" (Philippians 4:1).

- "Yea, and if I be offered upon the sacrifice and service of your faith, I joy, and rejoice with you all. For the same cause also do ye joy, and rejoice with me" (Philippians 2:17–18).

- "And the peace of God, which passeth all understanding, shall keep your hearts and minds through Christ Jesus" (Philippians 4:7).

- "I can do all things through Christ which strengtheneth me" (Philippians 4:13).

- "Rejoice in the Lord alway: and again I say, Rejoice" (Philippians 4:4).

Now get this: Paul was tossed into prison as an evil-doer. And those joyful sentiments you just read? *He wrote them while he was in prison.* Clearly, nothing is going to get Paul down. Just isn't going to happen. If that's not an example of pure joy, I don't know what is.

There are countless other examples of people who exude joy. Everyone wants it, and it seems everyone is trying to figure out how to get it. In fact, the results of several surveys show that 93 percent of all Americans want to experience more joy. Now, the almost universal desire for joy has launched a new style of marketing called "joy marketing"—a way to convince people they will feel joyful if they use a particular product.

Advertisers for the brands that have used joy marketing want to get their audiences to experience a specific emotion—joy—in response to their advertisements. They use sentimental images, inspiring quotes, and heartwarming slogans in an effort to connect with people on a profound, more meaningful level—one that encourages them to feel joy.

And it's working for a number of the brands that have tried joy marketing. Let's look at just a few of those marketing efforts you'll probably recognize.

One of the earliest efforts—in fact, it was launched before the term *joy marketing* was even coined—was Coca-Cola's feel-good campaign, "I'd like to buy the world a Coke." Maybe you remember those ads, and maybe you also remember how they made you feel. Well, you weren't alone: Coca-Cola not only received more than one hundred thousand letters praising the ad but also thousands of requests for the *sheet music* to the iconic jingle.

Bill Backer, the man who designed the campaign, said he started to see "a bottle of Coca-Cola as more than a drink . . . it was a tiny bit of commonality between all peoples, a universally liked formula." With that image in his imagination, he said, "I could see and hear a song that treated the whole world as if it were a person—a person the singer would like to help and get to know." Backer's idea worked, and Coke sales soared.

Another memorable stab at joy marketing was launched by ConAgra with a pair of campaigns: "Unleash the Joy" in 2013 and "Share the Joy" in 2015. ConAgra intended to position its product, Reddi-wip, as something that would help people create lasting, joyful moments. This one worked too: the company not only brought in higher monthly sales of the canned, sweetened whipped cream in all its varieties, but the campaign helped the company exceed its goal by increasing sales by more than 3 percent.

A "Christmas Miracle" campaign by the Canadian WestJet Airlines—a relative unknown—demonstrated that infusing joy into marketing created its own kind of miracle. In 2013, the company launched a campaign in which airline personnel handed out personalized Christmas gifts to unsuspecting flyers. Who could resist the joy in *that*? Sure enough, the campaign resulted in almost instant success: it was Canada's most shared viral ad of 2013 and one of the top five in the world. That's not all: an airline that was hardly a household name enjoyed more than forty million YouTube views of its advertisement, and sales skyrocketed 86 percent over the previous year.

Banking on the success of the 2013 campaign, WestJet launched a second campaign that capitalized on joy marketing in 2015. In the "12,000 Mini Miracles" campaign, airline employees set out to perform 12,000 random acts of kindness in a twenty-four-hour period, and another miracle was born.

And who can forget the effort by McDonald's to incorporate joy in not only its marketing but in the experience of its customers? Trying to rebound from its worst sales results in more than a decade, McDonald's dusted off its "I'm Lovin' It" campaign. You may remember that one: customers talked about their happiest moments in a McDonald's restaurant.

The new effort had to be bigger, better, and more effective, and this time company executives launched "Moments of Joy." The premise was simple: during the course of a single day, McDonald's set out to bring moments of joy to people in twenty-four cities across the world. Instead of just asking customers to *talk* about their happiest moments at McDonald's, the restaurant aimed to actually *create* joyful moments.

The result? People watching the ads experienced an emotional connection to McDonald's based on joy. It was just what the execs were looking for.

Part of the power of joy lies in what it does to your body. Researchers have found that joy causes specific physiological and biochemical alterations that enable you to better adapt to stress and become more resilient. That means you can feel profound joy no matter what is happening around you because joy doesn't depend on something good happening. Instead, it's an attitude of the heart or spirit.

Anyone alive knows that life involves a lot of risks. If you're afraid to take risks, you're sidelined by that fear: when you refuse to take risks you surrender the ability to move forward and to experience some really wonderful things. You stagnate. You merely exist. The most joyful people are those willing to take risks—sometimes big risks.

Joyful people know they may get hurt; they've all dealt with heartbreak, experienced sorrow, and felt betrayal. There's no doubt about it: those things hurt. But these things are part of living and loving and are well worth the risk. So go for it: don't be afraid of pain; you've faced it before, and you overcame it then. You'll overcome it again. And something really wonderful may happen in the interim, something you never would have experienced if you hadn't taken the risk. In his book *Invisible Monsters*, Chuck Palahniuk wrote, "The only way to find true happiness is to risk being completely cut open."

Along with knowing they may get hurt, joyful people know they may fail. We talked about failure and its importance in chapter 3. Comfort is a great thing when you're trying to fall asleep; otherwise, it's not a great long-term solution and can even result in depression. Get out there, take some risks, and give it your all. If you fail, get back up and try again. *That's* what counts. As Winston Churchill said, "Failure is not fatal: it is the courage to continue that counts."

When they take a risk and make a mistake or experience a failure, joyful people let it go—then start over. They don't allow the past to define them. They don't allow a mistake to dictate what they can or will do in the future. Yes, a mistake is a mistake. Yes, a mistake can be painful. But pretty much every mistake you ever make will help shape you into a better, stronger person—and that's definitely worth the risk.

Joyful people are optimistic about life in general, but they're also willing to face the truth. Unhappy things happen. In fact, downright ugly things happen. Periods of adversity will sink their talons in and shake you to your very core. It happens to everyone. People who are overly afraid of those things can get caught in denial—they'd rather ignore or deny something (to themselves *and* others) than face dreadful reality. And when you can't face what's happening, it's almost impossible to reinvent adversity to your advantage. Joyful people risk all the things associated with facing the truth, even when it's disappointing or hard. That's the only way to move past something hard and turn it into something better.

And joyful people accept and find ways to deal with change. You've undoubtedly heard the familiar adage, "Nothing is as constant as change." Change is inevitable. Most change is gradual, but some of it is sudden and unexpected. Some change is actually welcomed, while some is not—your spouse, parent, or child dies; your house burns down; you are fired or laid off from your job on a Friday afternoon. Along with change, one other thing is certain: our lives never stand still. Time marches on, and with that marching come the changes.

Joy can transcend all the changes. Joy can also be the loudest voice you hear, the one that shouts more exuberantly than the cries of adversity or sorrow. It is up to you to make sure joy is the voice to which you are listening, the one on which you are focusing. As one writer put it, "Both abundance and lack [of abundance] exist simultaneously in our lives, as parallel realities. It is always our conscious choice which secret garden we will tend . . . when we choose not to focus on what is missing from our lives but are grateful for the abundance that's present—love, health, family, friends, work, the joys of nature, and personal pursuits that bring us [joy]—the wasteland of illusion falls away and we experience heaven on earth."[46]

Change is inevitable; you don't have a choice, and you can't truly avoid it. If you're being forced into a change that seems overwhelming or threatening in any way, take the opportunity to review who you are, where you are going, and how you plan to get there. Doing so can help you embrace and accept change. It also literally puts you in place to reinvent your adversity and experience joy.

Once change is over, it's over. Accept it. Learn from your situation. Let go. Then move ahead to discover the new concept, idea, or thing that will inevitably bring purpose and meaning to your life. Chances are good it will be the same thing that bolsters your joy.

There are many simple things you can do to enhance your joy. Take opportunities to learn whenever you can; if you aren't in a position to take classes at a university or college, try community

---

46 Sarah Ban Breathnach, in John Cook, comp., *The Book of Positive Quotations*, 2nd ed. (Minneapolis, MN: Fairview Press, 2007), 342.

education classes, workshops, seminars—or books. Leap out of your comfort zone; move beyond the things that are familiar. Take one day at a time, and enjoy all the good each day has to offer. Keep mementoes, take pictures, or write in a journal to remember the things you especially relished; these are good things to pull out and look at when things start to get rough. You'll be reminded of how much you have to be joyful about.

Show gratitude. Appreciate the things you have instead of focusing on what you don't have. Look for the hidden blessings in the challenges you experience. Recognize the abundance in your life, even when you're in the middle of adversity. Try keeping a gratitude journal: every day, write down as many unique things as you can for which you're grateful. You'll be surprised at the things you have that will contribute to your joy.

As simple as it sounds, smile. Smile a lot. The very act of smiling stimulates your brain to produce endorphins, and endorphins make you feel good physically. It's a self-fulfilling prophecy of sorts, and it's free for the taking. The more you smile, the happier you'll be and the more inner joy you'll experience.

Notice your surroundings. You'll probably be surprised at all the places joy is hidden—you just need to be aware of them. If you want to experience consistent joy, be aware of what's going on around you. Stop often during the day, even when you're stuck in adversity, and ask yourself, *What is there to enjoy about this moment?*

Practice random acts of kindness. These don't have to be major productions; they can be as simple as letting someone go ahead of you in line, giving someone a compliment, calling a friend who is lonely, delivering a small basket to a shut-in, or running an errand for a busy neighbor. In 1982, a woman named Anne Herbert penned the following on a placemat in a restaurant in Sausalito, California: "Practice random acts of kindness and senseless acts of beauty." It's a formula that can contribute significantly to joy.

Get regular exercise. There are all sorts of benefits to exercise beyond getting and staying fit, and one of the best is the impact it has on your emotional well-being. Exercise boosts the levels of endorphins (the "feel-good" hormones) and reduces levels of the stress hormone cortisol. Regular exercise will stimulate your brain, lower your stress, reduce your pain, and increase feelings of joy. And whenever you can, take that exercise outside: scientists have found that spending time in nature improves your sleep, boosts your immune system, reduces your blood pressure, and lowers your stress levels.

Nurture the loving relationships in your life. Build a good support system by surrounding yourself with good friends and caring family members; gathering social support is one of the best things you can do to sustain you through adversity and help you as you work to reinvent that adversity.

Laugh loudly and often. Do something silly. Choose to be happy.

Finally, live in the moment and cherish the things that bring you even a brief respite from the chaos of adversity: a beautiful sunrise, a funny television commercial, a phone call from a friend, a baby's giggle, or a profusion of blooms outside your window. Look for these things. Appreciate them. Remember them when you need a reminder that things really are pretty terrific.

Ministering to the poorest of the poor in Calcutta, Mother Teresa spent her life in conditions that would try even the toughest of souls. She not only helped the poor and diseased and downtrodden, she lived among them. At the end of a lifetime of what some may have considered adversity, she wrote of the joy she experienced in helping others. "Joy is prayer;" she said, "joy is strength; joy is love; joy is a net of love by which you can catch souls."

American author and mountaineer Jon Krakauer perhaps put it best when he wrote:

> You are wrong if you think Joy emanates only or principally from human relationships. God has placed it all around us. It is in everything and anything we might experience. We just have to have the courage to turn against our habitual lifestyle and engage in unconventional living.
>
> My point is that you do not need me or anyone else around to bring this new kind of light in your life. It is simply waiting out there for you to grasp it, and all you have to do is reach for it. The only person you are fighting is yourself and your stubbornness to engage in new circumstances.

Chapter Seven

Giving: The Blessing of Life

For it is in giving that we receive.

—Francis of Assisi

A merican author Roy T. Bennett gave a snippet of advice that can literally change your life: "Learn to light a candle in the darkest moments of someone's life. Be the light that helps others see; it is what gives life its deepest significance."

Wait a minute, you may be thinking, *I'm the one going through the darkest moment of* my *life—and I'm supposed to worry about* someone else? Yes. You heard right.

At first blush, the very concept seems ridiculous. Completely crazy. But it's spot-on. When you are embroiled in the very real struggle of adversity, one of the most effective things you can do to reinvent your challenges is to reach out and really give to someone else. Because here's the secret about giving, as U.S. Secretary of Housing and Urban Development Ben Carson put it: "Happiness doesn't result from what we get, but from what we give."

It's a truth as old as time itself. In his farewell to the Ephesians, the Apostle Paul reminded them of "the words of the Lord Jesus, how he said, It is more blessed to give than to receive" (Acts 20:35). As the dictionary defines it, to *give* is to freely transfer something to someone else—to present with, provide with, supply with, furnish with. And here's the real basis of giving: it's something you provide *without the expectation of payment or anything in return.* It is done freely, without ulterior motive. It comes from the heart.

I learned about giving at a very young age from a mother who saw beyond our poverty to how we could bless the lives of others. What happened every Sunday was just one example of that. Though she couldn't take us herself, she wanted to make sure we grew up in the church, so she enlisted the help of a church official we affectionately called "Mr. Jack." Every week he picked us up and took us to Sunday school. And every week, poor as we were, my mother tucked into my hand three coins: a nickel for the collection plate and two pennies to spend at the corner store, where Mr. Jack took us after church. (Incredible as it seems, two cents bought a pretty exciting treat in those days.)

You can guess what often happened at first, while I was away from the all-pervading gaze of my mother's watchful eye: there were lots of times when I dropped the *pennies* in the collection plate and kept the nickel to spend on treats. But even in those earliest years, my mother's careful lesson penetrated my heart, and from the time I was a little girl, I always looked for someone in need with whom I could share.

My mother's simple act of sacrificing those three coins in the midst of her own poverty shaped my life—a life I knew I wanted to spend helping and giving to others. And that commitment didn't wane during all the times I found myself battered by adversity. I learned from my mother's powerful example the verity of what Winston Churchill meant when he said, "We make a living by what we get. We make a life by what we give."

My mother's was an example that stayed with me through thick and thin, and one that remains with me to this day. As my brother so humorously observed, I was the one who was always "picking up strays." And that simple habit, I found, had the power to carry me through some of the toughest periods of my life. At times when I could have felt helpless or hopeless beneath the magnitude of my own struggles, I found, as Charles Dickens wrote, "No one is useless in this world who lightens the burdens of others."

You may look at your situation and believe with all your heart that right at this minute, in your very real battle for survival, you have nothing much to give—that your exertion in moving from one day to the next is exhausting all your resources and leaving you without a shred of anything meaningful to share with someone else. Believe me when I tell you that no matter how hard things are today, you are *not* without the ability to give. Believe me when I say that no matter how hard you're scraping the bottom of the barrel, you are *not* without something to share. And believe me when I tell you that the very act of giving is one of the most effective things you can do to move beyond whatever anguish you are facing.

Believe me when I say all those things, because I have lived them.

Here's the real secret: *giving* doesn't have to involve a monumental contribution. In fact, it doesn't have to involve a tangible item at all. As the visionary Kahlil Gibran wrote in *The Prophet*, "You give but little when you give of your possessions. It is when you give of yourself that you truly give." The key to giving is to move outside your own world of concerns and to focus on what you can do for someone else, even when you're facing the toughest situation.

There are many examples of small and simple gifts that touch hearts and change lives—and some of them have gone viral on the internet, testifying to the power of giving. One man spends his lunch hour reading to an illiterate coworker; together they have discovered worlds beyond their own. A third grader battling a terminal illness spends hours with her crayons, drawing beautiful rainbows she hands out to people who look sad. A fourteen-year-old boy stomped out a message in the snow on the roof of a parking terrace outside the window where his mother was undergoing chemotherapy; it read, simply, "Hi, Mom. God bless."

When a boy's best friend was quarantined at a hospital, the seventh grader dropped by every day after school to play video games with him from outside the "bubble." A man struggling to make ends meet saved old bagels from the bakery where he worked and distributed them to the hungry people he met on his way home every day. When the mercury climbed above 103, two little girls waited anxiously for the garbage men so they could give them some ice-cold lemonade. And when an eight-year-old girl with leukemia who had only two weeks to live expressed the desire to hear Christmas carolers, literally thousands of people in her community surrounded her house to sing—not in the frosty snow but in the middle of June.

It doesn't take much to make a difference. Imagine the delight of the child upon discovering a gumball machine with two quarters taped to it. The accompanying note read, "Be generous—feels good, doesn't it?" Then there was the elderly woman who was sweeping a cluttered island between a Manhattan bike lane and the sidewalk. When asked what she was doing, she replied, "The city has so much to do; sometimes they can't get to everything. So I like to help." And "help" doesn't have to cost a dime: when an autistic boy was suspended for wearing a banana costume to a high school football game, the seasoned television news reporter who covered the story showed up in a grape costume as a show of support.

The simple act of giving can even extend to our animal friends. An elderly man whose dog can't walk anymore still takes her for a walk every day—in a wheelchair. An eight-year-old girl celebrated her birthday with her friends at a popular pizza restaurant—but instead of gifts, she asked her friends to bring items that could be donated to an animal shelter (food, blankets, towels, or cat litter). And a couple who lost their beloved dog, Phoebe, left a bin of tennis balls on the beach with a picture of their dog on a sign that read, "In loving memory of Phoebe. Please help yourself to a tennis ball for your dog to enjoy. You may wish to pop it back in the box afterward for another pooch to enjoy. Remember to live each moment just like your dog: with unconditional love, loyalty, and happiness."

It's often not the monetary value of a gift but the thought and time invested in it that makes it of such value to both giver and receiver. A beautiful example is the high school graduate whose father gave her one of her favorite childhood books: *Oh, the Places You'll Go!* by Dr. Seuss. From the time she entered kindergarten—over a period of thirteen years—her father had secretly asked every teacher, coach, and principal to write in the book a message to this girl expressing their belief in her and the things she could accomplish. It remains one of her most treasured possessions for many reasons, not the least of which is what it represents: visible evidence that she was front and center in her father's thoughts for more than a decade.

Even among these examples, in the simplest and most modest of gifts, we find testimony of why it is, as Jesus taught, more blessed to give than to receive. There are a number of reasons why that beatitude—possibly the least believed in the Bible—is so true.

In the first place—and we can make no mistake about this—we are expected to give. God expects it, and Jesus expects it. In teaching His disciples about giving, Jesus said "*when* you give," not "*if* you give" (see Matthew 6:2). That scarcely seems like optional instruction. In this, as in all other things, the Lord is clear on what He expects us to do.

We are also told we need to give for the right reasons. It is especially in giving what is most difficult, or *when* it is most difficult, that we become most like Him. During our adversity, when we are most tempted to look only inward, we can be most blessed by our efforts to consider others. We are warned, "He that observeth the wind shall not sow; and he that regardeth the clouds shall not reap" (Ecclesiastes 11:4). It is in reaching out during our adversity, in providing to someone else, that we take our focus off the winds and the clouds buffeting us so ferociously. Only by moving beyond our own hardship in reaching out to others are we able to sow and subsequently reap, for us *and* for them.

Giving is essential, but so is the *way* in which we give. During my earlier days of giving, I thought the recipients would appreciate me for giving. I thought for certain they would be grateful for my generosity. When they instead acted as if I were required to give and they were not the least bit happy with my thoughtfulness, I was filled with pain and agony. It took me a minute to understand that some people are unhappy no matter what you do. As I learned through those experiences, you can't get involved on that level. All you can do is just keep on giving.

Do we give so that others will see what we're doing and praise our efforts? Or do we give quietly and even anonymously, knowing that God—who, after all, is the one who matters most—will recognize the gift? Jesus's warning to His disciples was clear: "Take heed that ye do not your alms before men, to be seen of them: otherwise ye have no reward of your Father which is in heaven. . . . But when thou doest alms, let not thy left hand know what thy right hand doeth: That thine alms may be in secret: and thy Father which seeth in secret himself shall reward thee openly" (Matthew 6:1–4).

In His perfect way, God has set the example for us in terms of giving. We are told, "Every good gift and every perfect gift is from above" (James 1:17), leaving us no room to doubt that He is a God well exercised in giving. Clearly, His greatest—but far from only—gift was that of His Son (see John 3:17). In our quest to follow His example, to become images of Him, giving can be the most sublime of measures.

Through His universal sacrifice and all He did during His ministry, Jesus Christ also set the bar for all of us in what it means to give. Speaking of Jesus, Paul wrote to the Saints at Corinth that "though he was rich, yet for your sakes he became poor, that ye through his poverty might be rich" (2 Corinthians 8:9). He also reminded them, and us, that our willingness to give is a way "to prove the sincerity of your love" (2 Corinthians 8:8).

The scriptures leave no doubt as to what is expected of us when we are told that "God loveth a cheerful giver" (2 Corinthians 9:7). The Lord clearly takes special joy in one who gives with energy and delight, like the little girl who fashions rainbows and the man who reads to an illiterate coworker.

The commandment that we are to give is repeated throughout holy writ. God has even taken careful measure to tell us what our *attitude* should be in our giving: with the admonition that God loves a cheerful giver, we are also told, "So let him give; not grudgingly, or of necessity" (2 Corinthians 9:7). When we give indifferently or grudgingly or because we feel forced, it is as though the gift was not given. Doesn't that mean in God's eyes, giving is not optional? No, for obedience to every commandment is always up to us. While God requires that we give, our gift should always be willingly given. It is then that the blessings come.

Perhaps the blessings from giving come partly because giving refines our trust in God to provide for us—especially in times when we are most challenged. Maybe all you have left is a few crumbs, and you wonder what good those few crumbs could possibly do for someone else, especially when it's *all you have left*. That kind of giving can result in real fear if you're not careful—you can worry that you will no longer have enough if you give. But we are assured by a loving God that if we give even those few crumbs (whether they be crumbs of substance or crumbs of time and energy and love), we will receive in return (see Ecclesiastes 11:1). There is no doubt that blessings come to both giver *and* receiver.

When it comes right down to it, in fact, giving is an act of worship. Ultimately, the gifts we give are to an all-seeing and all-knowing God. Those coins I dropped in the collection plate (the pennies at first, and later the nickels) were my childish way of saying, "You've given me a lot, and here's something I can give back to you." I wasn't simply adding a few cents to the church budget; I was sending my thanks heavenward. The man who saves bagels and gives them to hungry people is saying, "I am so grateful for all You have given me, and I want to give what I can to Your children as a way of expressing my thanks." His is an act of real worship.

We may ask ourselves, *especially* in our extremities, "What shall I render unto the Lord for all his benefits toward me?" (Psalms

116:12). Our greatest purpose and goal in giving is to please the Lord—not for fame or the praise of man. We are blessed that along with it comes an amazing blessing for *us*: that of helping us move beyond the difficulties of adversity.

As we consider the gifts we may give—whether they be coins in a collection plate, June voices raised in Christmas caroling, a donation to a favorite charity, or a loving message stomped out in the snow—we should always remember the way God gives. The scriptures tell us that God "dispersed abroad; he hath given to the poor: his righteousness remaineth for ever" (2 Corinthians 9:9). When God gives, He gives generously and liberally. As followers of Christ, we would do well to follow His example. We clearly do not have what God has to give, but we can mirror His intent—which is described by *Unger's Bible Dictionary* as "a generous disposition of mind, resulting in large giving."

In our day, we have some stunning examples of "large giving"—according to *Business Insider*,[47] twenty of the richest people in the world are also the twenty top philanthropists. Some have *given away* more money than they currently have; all have spent a lifetime following the creed of pioneering American philanthropist Andrew Carnegie: "No man can become rich without himself enriching others. The man who dies rich dies disgraced."

The generosity of this "large giving" has extended to hundreds of people and organizations, enriching the lives of countless souls

---

47 See Tanza Loudenback and Emmie Martin, "The 20 Most Generous People in the World," *Business Insider*, October 12, 2015.

who have been touched directly or indirectly by "bread crumbs cast upon the waters." Together, these twenty have donated $106.8 billion to a variety of causes. Let's look at a few of them;[48] some will be familiar names, but others may be those you don't yet know. Your wallet may pale in comparison, but you will likely catch the spirit of what can be done by people of any means.

German IT entrepreneur Dietmar Hopp founded a multi-national company that provides analytics software to enterprises worldwide. Two decades ago, he established a foundation in his hometown that supports local education, sports, and health causes—including a university hospital and a pioneering facility for stem-cell research and practicing experimental medicine. To date, Hopp has donated $1 billion to the foundation—a sixth of his current wealth.

Another entrepreneur who has donated a sixth of his wealth is Paris-born Iranian-American Pierre Omidyar, the cofounder and current chairman of eBay. In 1998, he and his wife established a foundation that donates to a diverse range of causes, including entrepreneurship, human rights, food and energy, and games and technology. Six years ago, the pair pledged to donate most of their wealth to charities. Three years ago, Omidyar sold 10 percent of his shares in eBay to undisclosed charities, a stock gift valued at nearly $270 million.

Estimated to have donated fully half of his wealth over his life-time, Azim Premji—chairman of the Indian consulting and IT company Wipro—has spent his fortune to reform India's school

---

48 Examples excerpted and summarized from Loudenback and Martin.

and examination systems. His donations have provided computer training in eighteen languages and financed a university that awards degrees in teacher training.

Former CEO of Turner Broadcasting System and director of AOL Time Warner, magnate Ted Turner has given away more than half his wealth to community development and environmental and wildlife conservation causes. He donated $1 billion to the UN Foundation alone, an organization that promotes causes related to children's health, world peace, security, the environment, and women.

Chemical product manufacturer Jon Huntsman Sr., four-time cancer survivor, has donated more than $1.2 billion over his career, much of it to colleges and cancer-research centers. His generosity also established the Huntsman Cancer Institute at the University of Utah, a cutting-edge research and treatment center—the only cancer institute in the world designed by a patient and one that provides hope to thousands of cancer patients a year. His remaining wealth is estimated at $940 million, meaning he has given away 128 percent of his assets.

George Soros, the retired founder of Soros Fund Management, now spends his time serving as chairman of the Open Society Foundations, a network of charities to which he has donated $8 billion and which fund health, education, social services, community development, and international causes. The foundation is best known for its focus on human rights. His first project with the organization involved providing scholarships to black South Africans who were struggling under apartheid.

Retired CEO of one of the largest and most successful hedge-fund companies in the world, James Simons used a large percentage of his wealth to establish an education foundation before establishing two additional charities in memory of two deceased sons. The Nick Simons Foundation trains rural health-care workers in Nepal as well as funds humanitarian and social causes; the Paul Simons Foundation finances social and educational causes. Simons has also donated $30 million to autism research, with a pledge to donate $100 million in additional funds.

Facebook founder Mark Zuckerberg is one of the youngest self-made billionaires in the world and has promised to donate at least half of the wealth he accumulates over his lifetime. Recent donations included $75 million to San Francisco General Hospital and $25 million to aid in the fight against Ebola. With an ongoing commitment to education, Zuckerberg and his wife donated $100 million in Facebook shares to a public school system in New Jersey and $120 million to improve schools in California's Bay Area.

Then there are the computer darlings. Michael Dell, chairman and CEO of Dell Computer, directs a charitable foundation through which he has donated $1.1 billion to education, social and human services, arts and culture, and community development projects; he has also pledged $25 million to fund construction of a new teaching hospital in Austin, Texas, the corporate headquarters of Dell. Paul Allen, cofounder of Microsoft, has given $2 billion to global health causes, an additional $7 million in grants to Alzheimer's research, and $4 million to a conservation project focused on the preservation of sharks worldwide. His Microsoft cofounder, Bill Gates, now focuses on philanthropy, running the Bill & Melinda Gates Foundation and funding grants for agricultural development, urban poverty, global health, education, libraries, and emergency relief. He has heavily financed the World Health Organization; the Global Fund to Fight AIDS, Tuberculosis, and Malaria; and UNICEF, among others.

Warren Buffett—chairman and CEO of Berkshire Hathaway—is one of the wealthiest people in the world, but he's also one of the most generous. He donated fully 85 percent of his wealth to the Bill & Melinda Gates Foundation and partnered with Gates in creating the Giving Pledge. Under their direction, the program commits wealthy individuals to donate a large percentage of their wealth to charities and charitable causes.

Finally, known as the "James Bond of philanthropy," retail tycoon Charles Francis Feeney is on a mission to give away his entire fortune—and, having given away $6.3 billion with only $1.5 million to go, he has almost succeeded in achieving that goal. His foundation supports science, health care, education, and civil-rights causes in several countries, including the United States, Bermuda, and Vietnam.

There you have it—examples of generosity, of "large giving," that absolutely boggle the mind. No one could argue that all of them give liberally, and they are certainly models worth emulating. But few of us have those kinds of resources. How, then, do we give "liberally"?

It's worth our attention to look at scriptural examples of people who used the resources they had to "give liberally." During a famine in Palestine, those impacted were in desperate need of help. That help came from an unlikely source: members of the churches in Macedonia sent generous gifts of personal aid to the starving and poverty-stricken people of Palestine even though they were poor themselves. The people in Macedonia were, as Paul described them, freely willing and acted with much urgency to minister to the Saints in Palestine. In fact, said Paul, they ministered both "according to their power" and "beyond their power" (2 Corinthians 8:3–4).

Did you fully appreciate what happened there? The Saints in Macedonia reached out willingly, with much urgency, to help those who were suffering—even though they themselves were suffering. They too were poor. And look at what happened to the people in Macedonia who were so giving: "In a great trial of affliction the abundance of their joy and their deep poverty abounded unto the riches of their liberality" (2 Corinthians 8:2).

They gave as much as they possibly could. And they were transported out of their own adversity—out of their *great trial of affliction*—as a result. They had been enriched by the Holy Spirit and by God's grace, and they were no longer burdened by their own sorrows. Paul held them up as examples who abounded in grace and who, though they were poor, became spiritually rich. At the root of it all was giving—and it was, as Mother Teresa said of us, not how much they gave but how much love they put into the giving.

How much, then, do we give? Are we expected to give all or more than what we have—to put ourselves at risk or in danger because of our giving?

No. Such would be foolish. While we are to be liberal in our giving, and while most of us can give much more than we do, we are not expected to give more than what we have. Paul clarified God's direction when he wrote to the Saints in Corinth that they needed "readiness" but were to give "that which ye have. For if there be first a willing mind, it is accepted according to that a man hath, and not according to that he hath not. For I mean not that other men be eased, and ye burdened" (2 Corinthians 8:11–13).

The expectations are clear. We are to be willing to give cheerfully, from the heart. We are to be ready to give when it is needed. And we are expected to give that which we have without going into debt or risking our own safety by giving what is not ours.

As we ponder how we can give, particularly in the throes of adversity, there is an unavoidable responsibility to contemplate God's role in our giving. Consider this: If we are willing to give liberally, God will provide us with what we need to give others: "He which soweth sparingly shall reap also sparingly; and he which soweth bountifully shall reap also bountifully. . . . So let him give; not grudgingly, or of necessity: for God loveth a cheerful giver. *And God is able to make all grace abound toward you; that ye, always having all sufficiency in all things, may abound to every good work*" (2 Corinthians 9:6–8; emphasis added).

As someone once said, "The desire to be generous and the *means* to be generous both come from God." Think about that. Perhaps God has given you much so that *you* can give much. To whom much is given, much is required. Your gifts and talents and abilities are uniquely yours, and you are expected to use all of them—your time, talents, energy, and all with which you have been blessed—to the benefit of those around you who need what you have to offer.

Make no mistake. If you are willing, if your heart is prepared to give liberally, God will provide the means for you to give. And for both those who give and those who receive, there should be gratitude expressed to God: "For all things are for your sakes, that the abundant grace might through the thanksgiving of many redound to the glory of God" (2 Corinthians 4:15).

It is up to us, then, to multiply the bread we cast out on the waters. It is up to us to find those who need our help. It is up to us to reach out, to go beyond our own isolated sphere of suffering, to help ease the anguish of others. It is one of the best ways to begin to reinvent adversity and step out of our own harsh conditions.

I'm hoping by now that your heart is willing and you are ready to reach out, to cast your bread on the waters, even if—and maybe *especially if*—you are mired in hardship yourself and trying to claw your way out. I hope, too, that you realize there are many ways to give other than simply opening your wallet or writing out a check. If it hasn't already, I hope that giving will start to come naturally to you, an instinctive part of how you move forward in life.

Giving comes in all shapes and sizes, from large-scale global efforts to individual gifts, and it should be easy to find something to suit your individual abilities, desires, and budget. Whether you are giving of your time, your talents, or your resources, identify a cause in which you are interested and determine the extent to which you can help. Let's say childhood hunger is something you have always felt passionate about. If you have liberal resources, you may travel overseas with an organized group to feed starving children in an impoverished nation. With much more modest means, you can sponsor a hungry child who lives in another country. If you have little in the way of money to donate, you can always volunteer one day a month stocking shelves at a local food pantry or serving meals in a local soup kitchen.

With your giving, with every crumb of bread you cast out on the waters, you are making a powerful statement: you refuse to cave in. You refuse to be defeated by adversity. You have whatever it takes to face your problems head-on, and you will use whatever resources you can to lighten the load of another.

Be honest in your assessment of what God has blessed you with. Be realistic about which of those gifts you can use to bless another. You can become an instrument in God's hands even in the midst of your deepest trials. And as you do, you will be given the strength to complete your own journey, to arrive in your own promised land.

And here's the best part as summed up in a short, sweet statement by diarist Anne Frank: "How wonderful it is that nobody need wait a single moment before starting to improve the world."

Chapter Eight

Run the Race to the Finish

When you get into a tight place and everything goes
against you, till it seems as though you could not
hang on a minute longer, never give up then,
for that is just the place and time that the tide will turn.

—*Harriet Beecher Stowe*

My grandmother, one of the greatest influences in my life, used to quote the lyrics to a well-loved gospel song whenever she found herself in a difficult situation. I can still hear the tone in her quiet but determined voice as she said, "I believe I will run on and see what the end will be."

Her words touched my heart and penetrated my soul because they came from someone so dear to me, not because I understood their meaning or related to their sentiment. After all, the adults around me at that time made a great effort to protect me from the misfortunes of everyday life—the things by which they were almost constantly battered. Only when I grew and started to see the injuries in their lives (and mine) did I appreciate my grand-mother's absolute refusal to quit.

And now, having ridden one wave of adversity after another, I celebrate not only those inspired lyrics but something even greater. I know now from firsthand experience that the minute you refuse to quit is the minute you harness the lessons you've learned through adversity into a resolve to create a new future.

Refusing to quit is what empowers you.

If you want an example of someone who was empowered by the refusal to give up, look at Winston Churchill, who led Britain through the dark days of World War II. After retiring, he was invited to speak at the school he had attended as a boy. Before Churchill arrived, the headmaster told the students that the great-est countryman of their time "is going to come to this school, and I want every one of you to be here with your notebooks. I want you to write down what he says, because his speech will be something for you to remember all your lives."

When the elderly statesman arrived and was introduced to the students, his glasses were down on the end of his nose, as they char-acteristically were. He stood and repeated the immortal words he had once delivered to Parliament—words that energized a nation and then the world to fight against encroaching evil. His entire speech, unmatched in even our day, consisted of only five words: "Never, never, never give up." Five words. And then he sat down.[49]

---

49 See "These Are Great Days," in Charles Eada, ed., *War Speeches* (Boston: Little, Brown, and Company, 1942), 268–88.

No boy who heard Churchill that day ever forgot those five stirring words. And I hope you never forget them either. Regardless of the discouragement, disappointment, temptation, frustration, sorrow, or difficulty you face, never, never, never give up.

As my grandmother said so many times, run on and see what the end will be. Keep going, even when you're not sure you can continue to run, because you want to be there when the tide turns. You want to be there knowing you have come through the tough times—have risen above the difficulties to meet your objectives and achieve your dreams. The Reverend Jesse Jackson summed it up beautifully when he said, "If you fall behind, run faster. Never give up, never surrender, and rise up against the odds."

Never give up. Run on, as my grandmother said—run the race to the finish. Run faster if you fall behind. Keep pushing and struggling and trying, even during those times when you may have lost sight of exactly what you're trying for. Because you'll see it again, and when you do, it will be with new clarity and greater resolve. And before you know it, that vision will be your reality.

When you're fighting adversity, something odd often happens: just when you need them most, you find that the people around you start dropping like flies. Instead of rallying in support, they may even try to discourage you, telling you you'll never make it (remember Job?). Saying you may as well give up. Telling you it's useless to keep banging your head against the wall. (Try telling *that* to a woodpecker.) Don't listen to them; shake off the ones who are trying to pull you down. Keep slogging through the mud and slime and torrential downpour knowing you're moving toward something better than you've ever known before.

When you keep moving despite it all, you'll find that the ones who tried to hold you back are now the ones getting out of your way. Because, as self-improvement guru Dale Carnegie wrote, "Most of the important things in the world have been accomplished by people who have kept on trying when there seemed to be no hope at all." Even if you're the only one clinging to a shred of hope, cling to it with all your might.

Sometimes you'll feel vulnerable. Sometimes you'll doubt yourself. Sometimes you'll feel the icy fingers of fear clutching at every cell in your body. You may even feel like those awful dreams we all have—you know, the ones where you're in a public place wearing nothing but your underwear. No worries. If that's how you feel, imagine you're decked out in the most expensive, exotic underwear imaginable, and keep on going with your head held high. You won't be the first—or the last—to reach the finish line in nothing but your underpants.

Just remember: the only failure is in no longer trying. As baseball great Babe Ruth once said, "You just can't beat the person who won't give up."

As human beings, we are born with the instinct to never give up. Don't believe me? Just watch a baby. Babies scream and cry until they get what they want—and they never stop screaming or crying until they *do* get what they want. Somewhere along the way, that instinct gets buried in the propriety and decorum and expectations heaped on us by society. I'm not saying you should scream and cry until you get what you want; I *am* saying you should keep moving, pushing if you have to, until you come out of the melee and realize that you have, indeed, accomplished the impossible. Remember what Nelson Mandela said: something "always seems impossible until it's done."

In your journey through adversity and in your determination to never give up, you're going to learn a lot about perseverance. The main thing to realize about perseverance is that it's an active trait. It means you aggressively work instead of sitting idly by, waiting for something wonderful to happen or waiting for the problems to end. They won't—not on their own, that is. You have to put in the effort and do the work. But if you *do* make continuous effort and refuse to give up, the results can be remarkable:

> The line between failure and success is so fine that we scarcely know when we pass it; so fine that we are often on the line and do not know it. How many a man has thrown up his hands at a time when a little more effort, a little more patience would have achieved success? A little more persistence, a little more effort, and what seemed a hopeless failure may turn into a glorious success. . . . There is no defeat except within, no really insurmountable barrier save one's own inherent weakness of purpose.[50]

50 Jacob M. Brand, ed., *Second Encyclopedia* (Englewood Cliffs, NJ: Prentice Hall, 1957), 152.

There are many examples of perseverance in the scriptures, and one of the most compelling is that of Job. We've talked about him before, and you know the story. Job was a righteous man who loved the Lord and avoided evil. But talk about *adversity*—not much can rival all the things that hit him. He lost all his children: seven sons and three daughters. He lost his flocks and herds. In fact, he lost all his wealth. Then he was smitten with boils.

Instead of consoling him, his friends said his woes must be his fault—that he must have brought his miseries upon himself. Must have done something to anger God. Even his wife told him to give up, to "curse God, and die" (Job 2:9).

But Job? He was having none of it. Instead of cursing God, he did just the opposite, saying, "Blessed be the name of the Lord" (1:21). And try this on for size: he responded to all the naysayers by declaring, "Though [the Lord] slay me, yet will I trust in him. . . . He also shall be my salvation. . . . For I know that my redeemer liveth, and that he shall stand at the latter day upon the earth . . . yet in my flesh shall I see God" (13:15–16; 19:25–26).

Job refused to give up. He kept on fighting. He ran the race to the finish. Despite unrelenting opposition, he continued the course. And what did Job's astonishing perseverance bring him? In the end, the Lord blessed him with a family, great possessions, and good health. In the end, his fondest desire came to fruition—"mine eye seeth thee" (42:5).

Some of the greatest legacies the world has ever seen are the result of stubborn perseverance and the refusal to let adversity and its obstacles cause defeat. Ludwig von Beethoven was almost completely deaf when he wrote some of his greatest musical compositions. John Milton was blind when he wrote *Paradise Lost*. Military doctors of the day stridently resisted a female nurse, believing she would be a distraction to the men, but Florence Nightingale refused to give up and saved the lives of countless wounded soldiers. Abraham Lincoln was laughed at as a gangly, awkward country boy who failed at almost everything he tried, but he made one more go of it—and in doing so became one of the greatest U.S. presidents. Beethoven and Milton and Nightingale and Lincoln left indelible marks on the world not only because the Lord blessed them with various gifts but because they steadfastly persevered and refused to give up.

You may not have to face the same kind of opposition and obstacles Beethoven and Milton and Nightingale and Lincoln faced. But your trials and obstacles will feel every bit as sore while they are raging, and you will have to muster every bit as much perseverance and determination as they did in order to overcome the things you face. Let's look at a few others who ran the race to the finish despite tremendous odds and hardships that could have defeated those with lesser determination. I think it's important to look at what they did because their very grit gives each of us strength.

At the age of sixteen, Richard Branson was a high school dropout who wanted to start a student magazine. It failed. But he didn't let that failure stop him, even though he didn't have any of the traditional markers for success. Putting his nose to the grindstone, he established a mail-order record business; its success eventually led to the creation of Virgin Music, Virgin Atlantic, and Virgin Active. There was nothing easy about his road to success, though—on the way to his three lucrative enterprises, he tried and failed at many more, including Virgin Clothes, Virgin Cards, Virgin Vie, Virgin Vodka, and Virgin Cola. But he never, never, never gave up.

And I'm betting you've savored more than a few pieces of Hershey's chocolate. I'm also betting you have no idea of the blistering difficulties that faced Milton S. Hershey on his way to one of the greatest manufacturing empires in America. In fact, from the very beginning he faced difficulties that could have derailed him before he even got started. Throughout his childhood, his father's work required the family to move frequently, and his parents fought often.

Milton's father, Henry, wanted his son to become a man of letters, so he arranged for Milton to work as a printer's apprentice. Milton was miserable. In fact, he hated it so much he purposely threw his hat into the press and got himself fired.[51] Freed from the printing business, he pursued his real interest by landing a four-year apprenticeship with a candy maker in Lancaster, Pennsylvania. Henry was horrified, calling Milton's labor in the candy shop "women's work."[52] Undeterred, Milton finished the apprenticeship and opened his own candy business in 1867.

---

51 Michael D'Antonio, *Hershey: Milton S. Hershey's Extraordinary Life of Wealth, Empire, and Utopian Dreams* (New York: Simon & Schuster, 2006), 25.
52 Ibid.

Within a few years, Milton's parents were separated, and his mother, Fanny, directed most of her attention, energy, and aspirations toward Milton and his confectionary business. The pressures were great, the economy was flagging (it was the first of five years of the Depression), and within a few years, Milton's candy business failed.

Instead of giving up, Milton moved to Denver to reunite with his father—and to learn how to make better caramel. The confectioner for whom he worked taught him how to use milk, vanilla, and sugar instead of chewy paraffin in his caramels, and Milton perfected the recipe. With his caramel know-how but scarcely a dime in his pocket, he convinced his father to move with him to Chicago. From there, he went to New York.

The business climate in New York caught Milton unawares: he was still a small-time operation, and New York was moving ahead of the rest of the country in large-scale manufacturing. Milton worked tirelessly seven days a week to make candy for his own company; his mother and aunt moved to New York to help wrap the candies by hand.

Trying to diversify, Milton decided to produce sore-throat lozenges—but New Yorkers were steadfastly loyal to Smith Brothers Cough Drops. Smith Brothers had an advantage in addition to customer loyalty: they had pioneered a system of low-cost, low-wage production. Milton simply couldn't compete, and debt eventually forced him to close the business. He went crawling home to Pennsylvania penniless and with his tail between his legs but took with him the know-how to imitate the Smith Brothers' mass-production model, which would eventually lead to his success.

In Pennsylvania, he started making caramels and selling them out of a pushcart in Lancaster. The key to the success of his caramels was plenty of pasteurized milk, which gave his caramels a sweet, smooth, buttery taste. Milton's Lancaster Caramel Company then got a big break: a British importer visiting Lancaster fell in love with the caramels and placed a large order just as Milton's bank loan came due. It was a race to the finish for Milton to fill the order. From there, business exploded; by the early 1890s, the company filled a 450,000-square-foot factory on Church Street.

By 1900, Milton sold the Lancaster Caramel Company for $1 million—the equivalent of $27 million today. He had fallen in love with chocolate at the World's Columbia Expedition in Chicago, and he invested every dime in machinery to mass-produce the stuff. But don't think *that* was an easy road either: he loved chocolate but had no expertise with it, and he had to perfect his recipe through trial and error. He often burned both the milk and the sugar, even though teams of chemists and assistants toiled tirelessly in sixteen-hour shifts to help him get it right.

Through his unwavering resolve, the rest, as they say, is history. By 1912, Milton was a millionaire and visionary businessman who had built Hershey, Pennsylvania, into a utopian city focused on the business of chocolate. (And listen to this bit of good fortune: Milton had purchased a ticket on the *Titanic* but ended up being delayed by several days, so he wasn't on the ill-fated voyage.)

Then there's Henry John Heinz, the oldest of nine children born to German immigrant parents in 1844. At the age of eight, he was selling produce from his family's garden in Sharpsburg, Pennsylvania, to nearby neighbors; at ten, he loaded his wares into a wheelbarrow to expand his territory. By the time he was sixteen, he and several employees were making deliveries three times a week to Pittsburgh grocers.

After graduating from business college at the age of twenty-one, he became a partner in his father's brickyard, but his real interest was still in produce. A few years later, Henry formed a partnership to sell bottled horseradish—a business that soon expanded to include vinegar, sauerkraut, and pickles. In the chaos that followed the panic of 1873, Henry's business failed.

Determined to keep trying and to repay all his creditors, Henry formed another partnership, this time with his brother and cousin, and this time he added ketchup to the product line. Within a few years, the business prospered and was reorganized as the H. J. Heinz Company. Soon he was dubbed the "pickle king."

Henry started adding other products to his line—most famously tomato soup, and beans in tomato sauce. By 1892, the company offered more than sixty products, and it had the largest exhibit of any American food company at the 1893 World's Columbian Exposition in Chicago. By 1900, the company was first in the production of ketchup, pickles, mustard, and vinegar and fourth in the packing of olives.

Henry died at age seventy-five in 1919. But because he refused to give up when his horseradish company went belly-up, today's

H. J. Heinz Company manufactures thousands of food products in plants on six continents and markets them in more than two hundred countries and territories. It holds more than 50 percent of the market share in ketchup in the United States, more than 50 percent of the frozen-potato market with its Ore-Ida brand, and almost half of the nation's tuna market with its StarKist tuna. In all, the company has 150 number-one or number-two brands worldwide.

And don't forget Colonel Harland Sanders. After being fired from a string of jobs throughout his career—including tire salesman, fireman, insurance salesman, and cook—he finally started cooking chicken in 1930 at the age of forty. There was nothing luxurious about his accommodations: the Great Depression was in full force, and the colonel cooked his chicken out of his roadside Shell service station in rural Kentucky. There was actually no restaurant in his gas station, so he served the chicken in his personal living quarters, which were attached to the Shell station.

Over the next ten years, the colonel perfected his "secret recipe," which included a special blend of herbs and spices as well as a pressure-fryer cooking method. His chicken was widely praised, but, unfortunately, praise didn't pay the bills. When an interstate came through the rural Kentucky town where the colonel was selling his chicken in the 1950s, regular road traffic slowed to a crawl, and he was forced to close his business.

At the age of sixty-two, the colonel set out with a $105 Social Security check in his pocket. He'd never given up before, and he wasn't about to then. He hit the road in an effort to pitch his secret chicken recipe to restaurants, hoping to franchise it. He drove from one to the next, sleeping in his car, and was rejected by 1,009 restaurant owners. Some even told him he was crazy.

But he refused to give up. And on the 1,010th try, he found his first partner—someone willing to take a risk on his secret recipe. The risk paid off. That restaurant was in Salt Lake City, Utah, and became the first Kentucky Fried Chicken. Within a year, it tripled its sales, and 75 percent of its revenues came from the colonel's chicken. In 1974, at the age of seventy-four, Sanders sold his company—the one no one would initially even sneeze at—to a group of investors for $2 million.

Inspiring examples of people who refused to give up are found everywhere. When Paulo Coelho's book was finally published by an obscure Brazilian publishing house, the sales weren't promising. They were so bad, in fact, that the publishing house told him to give up. Instead of giving up, Coelho left Rio de Janeiro with his wife and spent forty days in the Mojave Desert in an effort to heal from the rejection.

One sentence in Coelho's book reads, "When you want something, the whole universe conspires to help you." Coelho wrote that sentence, and he believed in his book, which relates the story of an Andalusian shepherd boy who travels the world in search of earthly treasure. Determined to keep struggling, Coelho refused to give up. He decided to take matters into his own hands and started knocking on doors to sell his novel.

Today, that book, *The Alchemist*, has sold 65 million copies and has been on the *New York Times* best-seller list for more than 315 weeks. It has also been translated into eighty different languages, setting the Guinness World Record for the most translated book by any living author.

No one would ever have believed Emily Blunt would achieve any sort of success, especially in the movies: between age seven and fourteen, she was handicapped by such a severe stutter she was barely able to carry on a conversation. She was frustrated and haunted by the fact that she had a lot to say but couldn't manage to speak coherently.

Then her junior high teacher encouraged her to try out for the school play, an astonishing suggestion considering Blunt's inability to communicate. But with the teacher's gentle pressure and Blunt's own determination to not give up, she started trying character voices and accents to get the words out. It worked. By the time she graduated from high school, she had completely overcome her stutter.

Well-known for her roles on both the small and large screen, Blunt has been nominated for five Golden Globe Awards.

Sometimes unavoidable tragedy occurs and makes it seem like giving up is the only rational thing to do. When Shania Twain was only two, her parents divorced; she rarely saw her father, and her mother and stepfather—an abusive man who fought frequently with her mother—often couldn't make enough money to get by. When she was just eight years old, Shania started singing in bars to make extra money, trying to help support the family. Many times her mother woke her up at all hours of the night to get up and perform. But in addition to earning money, the music gave Shania much-needed solace from a very difficult childhood.

Shania's talent was recognized early on; when she was thirteen, she was featured on a talent show on CBC Television in Canada. During high school, she got the opportunity to sing with a local band. After graduating, she started taking lessons from a singing coach, joined a band called Flirt, and toured all over Ontario with the band.

But that all came to a screeching halt when Shania was just twenty-one and her mother and stepfather were killed in a head-on collision with a logging truck. After performing for fifteen years and starting a promising music career, she put everything on hold to care for her three younger siblings, who were teens at the time. Many told her it was time to simply give up—that there were too many obstacles and she'd never be able to break back into the music scene. But Shania refused to give up. Once her youngest brother graduated high school, she packed her meager possessions and headed for Nashville to try again.

Today, Shania Twain is one of the best-selling singers in Canada, second only to Celine Dion. Her album *Come On Over* is the best-selling country album of all time. Winner of multiple BMI songwriter awards, she is also a Grammy Award winner. Her fans have affectionately dubbed her the "queen of country pop."

Yet another singer who refused to give up is music success Katy Perry, who faced one failure after another on her way to stardom. Dropping out of high school at the end of her freshman year to pursue singing, she started out as a gospel singer due to the influence of her born-again Christian parents. Her first gospel album was a flop—it sold only two hundred copies before its producer, Red Hill Records, ceased operations and went out of business.

Switching to popular music, Perry moved to Los Angeles and signed with Island Def Jam. Within the year, her contract was terminated.

Refusing to give up, she landed a contract the next year with Columbia Records, which decided to make her the lead vocalist in a band called the Matrix. That success, unfortunately, was short-lived; Columbia simply shelved the project when it was 80 percent complete. Katy Perry was out on the streets again.

You'd think after being dropped from three labels in practically as many years, Perry would have given up and moved on to something else. But she was determined to run the race to the finish. Continuing to pursue her career, she worked at odd jobs to pay the rent and did backup vocals to stay visible. Finally, in 2006, she signed a contract with the newly formed Capitol Music Group. Shortly afterward, she had her first huge hit single, which launched her career as a commercial success.

Five songs from her album *Teenage Dream* topped the Billboard Hot 100 chart consecutively, making her the first woman to accomplish that feat. Michael Jackson is the only other artist to achieve that success. Her numerous awards include five American Music Awards, six Billboard Music Awards, six MTV Europe Music Awards, and five MTV Video Music Awards—all because she refused to give up.

I've given you a handful of examples of people who were determined to run the race to the finish. They refused to quit. There's another common thread in the tapestry of their lives that can help you come out of your adversity stronger, more capable, and with a brighter future. It's your refusal to crumble under pressure. Legendary World War II general George S. Patton beautifully summed things up when he said, "Pressure makes diamonds." And whether you emerge from your adversity in broken shards or formed into facets like a brilliant diamond depends on how you respond to the pressure.

One of the greatest gifts of adversity is pressure. And one of the greatest gifts of pressure is its ability to make of us diamonds. What happens between here and there can perhaps best be demonstrated in the world of sports, but it doesn't depend on your ability to run a marathon or shoot a three-point basket or sink a hole-in-one. It's your ability to perform in a high-pressure situation. Sports psychologist Martin Turner, an expert in human performance under pressure, said, "The key difference between those who get the Gold medal and those who don't is between the ears."[53]

What goes on between the ears is what enabled basketball great Kobe Bryant of the Los Angeles Lakers to score eighty-one points in a single NBA game against the Toronto Raptors. Lakers owner Jerry Buss said it was "like watching a miracle." That assessment may not have been far off: only Wilt Chamberlain ever scored

---

53 Amy Morin, "Why Successful People Don't Crumble Under Pressure," *Forbes*, August 7, 2014. The following sports-related information on standing up to pressure is adapted from Morin.

more points—one hundred, to be exact.[54] (Sadly, few people saw Chamberlain's astonishing performance, coming as it did at a sparsely attended 1962 game in Hershey, Pennsylvania.) Certainly, both Bryant and Chamberlain were gifted hoopsters, but it was what went on between their ears that made the difference.

What goes on between the ears is also what enabled golfer Rory McIlroy to make one of the greatest comebacks in sports history. In 2011, he was the second youngest player in contention for the Masters title and had a four-shot lead at twelve under as the final round began. He had owned the first three rounds, and fans and experts alike were ready to crown him the next star.

While his four-shot lead quickly disappeared, he still went into the back nine tied for the lead. It was a nail-biter until it all fell apart between the tenth and twelfth holes. Adding insult to injury, his ball splashed into Rae's Creek on the thirteenth. In the blink of an eye, McIlroy eliminated himself from contention, finishing with the worst final round in Masters history—eight over par. You read that right. He went from a solid lead to the worst final-round score in the history of the tournament—all because the pressure got to him.

That was it. He made history with his bad score at the Masters. Just months later, he made history again—this time at the U.S. Open where, at the age of twenty-two, he became the youngest U.S. Open winner since Bobby Jones in 1923. McIlroy's final score was sixteen under par, an amazing eight-stroke lead over his nearest competitor.

---

54 Mike Bresnahan, "Remembering the Night Kobe Bryant Scored 81 Points," *Los Angeles Times*, January 21, 2016.

Again, he swung the club with precision, but the magic happened between his ears. Interviewed after his history-making victory,
McIlroy alluded to his disappointing performance of a few months
earlier when he said, "I felt like I got over the Masters pretty quickly,
and I kept telling you guys that. I don't know if you believed me."[55]

Graeme McDowell, who won the U.S. Open the year before,
said of McIlroy, "Nothing this kid does ever surprises me. He's
the best player I've ever seen."[56] *What?* The best player he's ever
seen? Are we talking about the same guy who totally bombed the
Masters that year? Yes. We are. How is that possible? Because of
what goes on between the ears—the mindset he brought to the
game he won. Just like Bryant and Chamberlain, he clearly had
raw talent, but his mental game was what made the difference.

Why have I digressed to basketball and golf? Because the skills
that let these three amazing athletes thrive under pressure in the sports
world are the same traits that can help you thrive under the pressure
of adversity—traits that will help you reinvent your challenges and,
in the end, enable you to come out stronger and better. Here's what it
boils down to: how you perform in the pressure of adversity is dictated
by the mind.

The key is the ability to perform in high-pressure situations—
and if there's ever a situation marked by high pressure, it's adversity.
Your house burns to the ground. Your husband files for divorce.

---

55 "McIlroy Cruises to First Major Title, Makes History at U.S. Open," *Golf,* December 6,
2011.
56 Ibid.

You lose your business and go bankrupt. You're living in your car. Your child is diagnosed with cancer. *You* are diagnosed with cancer. Your world is turned upside down, and you're not sure how to make things right again. You're not even sure if things will *ever* be right again. *That's* pressure. And just like Bryant and Chamberlain and McIlroy, that's the time you need to perform.

A lot of it has to do with the way you perceive the adversity. If you see it as a threat, you run the risk of crumbling under the pressure. You feel anxious. Uncertain. Afraid. You agonize that you'll make a bad decision or do something really stupid. *Choke* author Sian Beilock calls it "paralysis by analysis"—you overthink so dramatically you're unable to do things you'd normally consider easy.[57] You worry you won't be able to perform, and pretty soon that becomes a self-fulfilling prophecy. Sure enough, you can't perform. Can't handle the simplest tasks. Instead of looking for successes, you find yourself looking for threats—and in any adverse situation, they're generally easy to find.

In the middle of it all, you're repeatedly telling yourself, *Don't fail. Don't mess up.* But as soon as that dialog starts going through your mind, it's all you can think of. And eventually, that's exactly what will happen. A famous experiment showed what goes down in the brain: a professor told a group of participants not to think about white bears. As soon as they concentrated on not thinking about white bears, that was all they could think about.[58]

---

57 See Morton.
58 Ibid.

When you get obsessed with the possibility of failure, that's where your focus is. Ultimately, you're more likely to fail. You crumble under pressure. Simple as that.

Let's consider the other scenario. If you are able to see adversity as a challenge, you're likely to have a completely different experience. You actually get excited about the challenge. You develop a positive mental approach to the pressure, and you are able to meet the demands of the situation. Your performance actually improves. You're able to concentrate, control your emotions, and make good decisions. As Turner explains it, "A challenge state reflects a positive mental approach to pressure situations where our mental resources meet the demands of the situation."[59]

Staying calm is an important part of staying strong under pressure, and new research at Harvard Business School shows that lots of us—especially while dealing with adversity—focus too much on calm as an end instead of on the things that lead to calm. It all goes back to the threat-versus-challenge idea. "People have a very strong intuition that trying to calm down is the best way to cope with their anxiety, but that can be very difficult and ineffective," explains the author of the study. "When people feel anxious and try to calm down, they are thinking about all the things that could go badly. When they are excited, they are thinking about how things could go well."[60]

---

59 Ibid.
60 Travis Bradberry, "How to Be Calm Under Pressure," *Forbes*, November 30, 2015.

The secret is to put things in perspective, to look at your adversity with energy and excitement, not with anxiety and dread.

Easy for you *to say*, you may be thinking. *In fact, the whole thing is easier said than done.* You're right. It *is* easier said than done. But not impossible. And it's something you are fully capable of doing. In the same way you manage anything else, there are some great tips to help you manage adversity by changing your perspective.[61]

Start by asking yourself an important question: How much will this matter in five years? If you're honest with yourself, you'll probably realize that much of your anxiety is tied to things you're anticipating, not things grounded in reality. Try to move past the dread you anticipate—public embarrassment is a big one—so you can start picking up the pieces.

You can also gain valuable perspective by thinking about situations worse than yours. Throughout this book I've shared a number of examples of people, many of them well-known, who have coped with incredibly difficult adversity. Remember? Franklin Delano Roosevelt was paralyzed from the waist down, an affliction he dealt with throughout his entire presidency. Vincent van Gogh never sold a painting until just before he died, but he kept at it. First grader Annie Clark has no arms. Babe Ruth struck out twice as often as he hit home runs. Malala Yousafzai was shot in the head when she advocated for the right of a child to an education. Abraham Lincoln lost every election he ever entered until that last one. Colonel Sanders hit the road at age sixty-two with $105 in his

---

61 The following tips are adapted from Bradberry.

pocket and slept in his car while he was rejected by more than a thousand restaurants. The biblical Job lost it all—wealth, possessions, family, and health; even his friends turned on him.

And here's the other thing I've shared: all of these people pulled out of their adversity. They went on to achieve remarkable things. If they did it, so can you. Remind yourself often and enthusiastically that you refuse to let this adversity define you—not now, not ever.

Another way to change your perspective is to stop worrying about what others think. It may be hard to believe this right now, but people *aren't* looking at you and thinking you're a total loser because of what you're dealing with. The powerful Eleanor Roosevelt said something I've always loved: "You wouldn't worry so much about what *others think of you* if you realized how seldom they do."

Still another way to gain proper perspective on what you're going through is to engage your logic. Try to stick to the facts. No right-thinking person would try to tell you adversity isn't difficult. It is. There's nothing fun or funny about it. It's extremely chaotic, and chaos can do funny things to your mind. You start to imagine the worst, and before long it's all you can see. Instead, ask yourself some important questions and try to stick to the facts. What exactly has happened? What are the possible repercussions? Is it possible to avoid some of those repercussions? If so, what do you need to do, and who do you need to involve? If not, how can you help reduce some of the damage?

Once you have your answers, make a plan. Confront things head-on. The longer you put it off, the worse things are bound to get. Do whatever you can to regain some of your power. Get excited about the possibility of rising from the ashes.

And whatever you do, don't be so hard on yourself. Nobody's perfect. Even the most brilliant people make mistakes. Remember Oprah Winfrey? She was fired from her first reporting job because she was deemed "unfit for television." And Walt Disney? He was fired from the *Kansas City Star* for his lack of creativity. Henry Ford's first car company failed after just eighteen months. See? As much as you feel like beating yourself up, it's a waste of valuable energy. It never accomplishes anything. It certainly doesn't make you calm. Focus on the things you can change and on what you want in your future.

I just reminded you of some of the people I've talked about in this book. I used them as examples because they all managed to reinvent their adversity, some in spectacular ways. But I also used them because I believe some of the greatest value in reading about the adversities of others is the realization that you are not alone. Just knowing you're not alone is often enough to kindle hope even in the most difficult circumstances. Author Anna White wrote, "I think this is what we all want to hear: that we are not alone in hitting the bottom, and that it is possible to come out of that place courageous, beautiful, and strong."

If you're sliding down a steep slope toward the bottom, or even if you've already hit the lowest point imaginable, it *is* possible to come out of where you are. And part of the reason is that you are never alone. There is always someone out there who has been where you are, who understands what it's like, and who is willing to reach out.

Sometimes the most damaging part of adversity is the isolation. The loneliness. The way it makes you feel you have been shoved away into a corner with the rest of the bad people—only *they're* not around either. You often feel all alone and like no one else understands what you are going through. And that even if a handful of people understood, no one cares enough to help.

Many may look at you, struggling through the chaos of your situation, unable to figure out why you don't do something to *help yourself*. What those people don't get is that there are days when it takes all your strength just to get out of bed.

But here's an important truth, and I need you to believe what I am about to say. No matter how isolated you feel, you are not alone. You may *feel* all alone, but you are not. You never have been, and you never will be.

You may feel broken, disconnected, alienated, distant from the people who mean the most to you. Those feelings can be very real, and you may feel convinced that you are, in very fact, alone. But those are only feelings. They are not reality. And you are not alone.

You may feel like crying. If you do, then cry. You may feel like screaming. If you do, then scream. Cry and scream until your pulse slows and your breathing becomes deep and cleansing. As it does, remember that you are not alone. There are others who have felt just like this. Others who have cried and screamed until all the tears dried up.

You may feel completely overwhelmed by the pressures and problems of your situation. You may think you are incapable of weathering this storm, whatever its intensity. You may not realize that at the depths of your soul is a storm cellar where you can wait out the fury, warm and safe. You are not alone.

You may be convinced you can't face one more complication, one more piece of collateral damage. But you can. I assure you that you can face whatever happens. Because you are not alone.

You may believe things will never be the same again. You may believe that even if you survive your current catastrophe, it will batter you beyond your ability to recover. Nothing is further from the truth. And you are not alone.

You may believe with all your heart—what's left of it, anyway—that you are too weak and too worn out and too exhausted to carry your burden any longer. But you are not alone; it's time to lay your burden down for a moment, regain your inner strength, pick it back up, and cross the finish line.

You may feel like your only option is to give up. I will once again borrow the words of the visionary Winston Churchill: "Never, never, never give up." Because you are not alone.

You are not alone because there are people going through the same thing. The details of their particular trials may be different from yours, but the things in their heart and soul echo yours. They can understand. They can help.

You are not alone because there are people you can talk to who know how to help. Find a member of the clergy, a counselor, a therapist, a mental health worker. Pour out your anguish, and apply the balm of Gilead.

You are not now, and never will be, alone. There is a God in His heavens who is keenly interested in you and who will reach out to bind up your aching heart.

Trust that you can get help; believe that everything in your life will eventually change for the better. You can learn and practice and master those feelings just like you can any other skill. And once you do, things will begin to change. Johann Wolfgang von Goethe provided a beacon of hope when he wrote, "As soon as you trust yourself, you will know how to live."

Along with trusting yourself, believe in yourself. Nothing will work out if you don't; *everything* will work out if you do. Remember the maxim of brilliant industrialist Henry Ford: "Whether you think you can, or you think you can't—you're right." Change your "perception," and change your life.

When it comes to adversity, there are two different kinds of people. There are the ones who reinvent adversity, who overcome even the most difficult things that could ever happen and who go on to experience a life of joy and prosperity. On the other side are the ones who crumble under pressure and surrender to defeat; they are defined by their adversity. The biggest difference between these two groups is not resources or opportunity or even intelligence. It's that they believe they can do it. The ones who come out on top believe they can. And they're right.

When you're in the middle of adversity, you may not be exactly sure where you're going. If you believe in yourself, you make the important decision to move forward anyway, believing you will figure it out. Colonel Sanders had to be pretty discouraged when after months of sleeping in his car and trying to peddle his chicken he wasn't making any progress. But he believed he would figure it out. And he did. Sidney Poitier was told he couldn't act, but he believed he would figure out a way to learn. And he did. Jay-Z was turned down by every record label but never lost his determination to release an album; he kept at it, believing he would figure out a way. And he did.

It doesn't cost you anything to believe in yourself, and it can result in incredible dividends. When you believe in yourself, you keep going. After being knocked down, you get up again and again and again because you know you can. You dust yourself off and get back to the business at hand. You never let failure wipe you out because you believe there is another way. And you are right.

To believe in yourself, count your wins. We all make mistakes, and we all fail. But we all do things right, too. So often we focus on the negative and forget the positive. Look at the good things you've done and remind yourself that even better things can happen down the road. Instead of engaging in negative self-talk, talk to yourself like the champion you are. Celebrate who you are and what you can do. And never let those things get lost—never lose the ability to hear your voice above the fracas just because the winds are howling. They'll stop. Please believe me on that. Because I have been in some absolute hurricanes of adversity, and the sun has never failed to come out again once the wind stops blowing. And it always stops.

So never give in, and never, never, never give up. Keep trying—until. Run on, as my grandmother said, and see what the end will be. Remember the advice of legendary coach Vince Lombardi: "Winners never quit, and quitters never win." Determine right now that you will win by knowing you will never quit—by knowing you will run the race to the finish.

Be prepared to move from agony to achievement because it is firmly within your ability to do so. I want to send you to the finish line with the stirring words of spiritual teacher and author Marianne Williamson because in them you will harvest the courage to take you all the way:

> Our deepest fear is not that we are inadequate. Our deepest fear is that we are powerful beyond measure. It is our light, not our darkness, that most frightens us. We ask ourselves, "Who am I to be brilliant, gorgeous, talented, fabulous?" Actually, who are you not to be?

Foundations, Funds, and Charities

In Chapter 7 (Giving: The Blessing of Life) we explore the essential key to overcoming our own problems by helping others. Many of the people whose amazing stories are shared throughout *Emotional Emancipation* used this secret as they overcame their own adversity. When they broke free of their problems and created a positive life for themselves, they often went on to create their own foundations or charities to "pay it forward" and help others lift themselves up.

Following is a list of organizations created by or supported by some of the indomitable people featured in this book who give hope to countless people around the world. In your own journey to joy and hope, consider supporting one of these charities or find other creative ways to help lift those around you.

African National Congress Youth League
Alzheimer's Association
The Angel Network
Cedars-Sinai Medical Center
Celebrity Fight Night Foundation
Charity Projects Entertainment Fund
The Charlize Theron Africa Outreach Project
Children's Hospice & Palliative Care Coalition
Chrysalis
Diana, Princess of Wales Memorial Fund

Entertainment Industry Foundation

The Friars Foundation

Friends of Bethany

The Fulfillment Fund

The Gates Foundation

Global Fund

Global Poverty Project

Help for Heroes and Global Angels

Hollywood Education and Literacy Project,

Human Rights Campaign

The James Jordan Boys and Girls Club

Kristen Ann Carr Fund

Legacy of Hope

Legacy of Hope Foundation

Make a Wish Foundation

The Malala Fund

The Mark Wahlberg Foundation

The Marshall Mathers Foundation

The Michael J. Fox Foundation

The Milagro Foundation

Motion Picture and Television Fund Foundation

NAACP

National Veterans Foundation

Not on Our Watch Foundation

The Omidyar Network

The Oprah Winfrey Foundation

PlayPumps

Project HOME and Unite for Japan
Reach for a Dream Foundation
Reach for a Dream Foundation,
Soles4Souls
Special Olympics
Spirit of Women Health Network
St. Jude Children's Research Hospital
The Stephen and Tabitha King Foundation
Together for Short Lives
UNHCR
UNICEF
United Cerebral Palsy
United Nations Foundation
The Walt Disney Company Foundation
Whatever It Takes
The Will and Jada Smith Family Foundation
Women's Fund for Scotland
World Vision

Corporations that Support Women's Empowerment and Advancement

The message of Chapter Four (Vision: The Ability to See the Invisible and Achieve the Impossible) is that it's possible to create a better future, and it starts by being able to imagine that future. Throughout history, there have always been people with the vision that they could make the world a better place, and that energized them to achieve their goals. The corporations listed below are a selection of companies that have demonstrated a commitment to the ideals of Emotional Emancipation, especially the empowerment and advancement of women in the workplace.

Accenture

Access Bank

Air France

Alcatel-Lucent

Allens

The Anita Borg Institute for Women and Technology

Astellas

Avon Products

Barclays Group

The Body Shop

BPW International

The Brazilian Post and Telegraph Corporation

CA Technologies

CAIXA

Calvert Investments

Cisco Systems

Citigroup

The Coca-Cola Company

Compania de Tierras Sud Argentino

Contigo

Deloitte Touche Tohmatsu (DTT)

Denmor

DOW Chemical Company (USA)

Eletrobras Eletrosul

Ethiopian Airlines

ExxonMobil

FCC

Franky and Ricky

Gap, Inc

Gender and Technology EQUAL Development Bank

Gender Equality Model Egypt ("GEME")

General Motors

The Goldman Sachs Group, Inc

Groscon Administradora de Consorcios LTDA

HCL

HSBC

The Hydroelectric Company of Sao Francisco (Chesf)

IBERDROLA

IKEA Women's Empowerment Program in India

Intel

ITAIPU Binacional

Jaguar and Land Rover

Johnson & Johnson

Kellogg Company

Kraft Foods

Levi Strauss & Co

L'Oreal

Macy's

Mars Chocolate

Mary Kay Inc

Merck

Micato Safaris

National Bank Australia

Natura

Newmont Mining

New Space

Novo Nordisk

PaxWorld Management LLC

Primark

Proctor & Gamble

Repsol YPF

Rio Tinto

Schneider Electric Brazil

Scotiabank Canada

Scotiabank Mexico

Sodexo Inc.

Standard Chartered

Sun Microsystems

Symantec Corporation

Tag Heuer

Total

Truckers Against Trafficking

Tupperware

Unilever

United Nations Federal Credit Union (UNFCU)

Yahoo!

About the Author

Dr. Dee Carroll, PhD, is a much sought-after speaker, coach, seminar host, and consultant. Her clients include Washington Headquarters Services, the Department of State, the Executive Office of the President, Georgetown University, and many others.

She holds degrees in psychology, business administration, and management and has founded a multimillion-dollar firm.

Additionally, she has appeared before the United States Senate Committee on Housing and Urban Affairs, been featured in a number of publications, and has appeared on several television and radio programs, including CNN. She has lectured nationally and internationally and has been a guest lecturer at both Howard and Bowie State Universities.

Visit Dr. Carroll at www.drdeecarroll.com for more information on her work as an inspirational speaker, for additional tips, such as "30 Second Quick Fixes for Reinventing Yourself," and for advice on how to take your initial steps toward emotional emancipation.

If you are interested in:

*having Dr. Dee teach an Emotional Emancipation Course at your organization
*ordering copies of Emotional Emancipation for your organization ($16.99 + $3.99 S&H per book, bulk discounts may be available)
*joining Dr. Dee's mailing list for motivational articles, newsletters, and special offers

Please include:

name: _____

organization name: _____

telephone number: _____

email address: _____

website: _____

shipping address: _____

Contact Dr. Dee at: contact@drdeecarroll.com
visit her website: www.drdeecarroll.com

Made in the USA
San Bernardino, CA
21 November 2018